THE ENGLISH WARS AND REPUBLIC, 1637–1660

who were the Levellers?

G. E. SEEL

ROUTLEDGE

London and New York

First published 1999 by Routledge
11 New Fetter Lane, London EC4P 4EE

Simultaneously published in the USA and Canada
by Routledge
29 West 35th Street, New York, NY 10001

Routledge is an imprint of the Taylor & Francis Group

Typeset in Grotesque and Perpetua
by Keystroke, Jacaranda Lodge, Wolverhampton
Printed and bound in Great Britain by St Edmundsbury Press,
Bury St Edmunds, Suffolk

British Library Cataloguing in Publication Data
A catalogue record for this book is available from the British Library

Library of Congress Cataloging in Publication Data
Seel, Graham E., 1963–
    The English Wars and Republic, 1637–1660 / G. E. Seel.
        p.   cm. – (Questions and analysis in history)
    Includes bibliographical references and index.
    ISBN 0–415–19902–6 (pb)
        1. Great Britain–History–Puritan Revolution, 1642–1660.
    2. Great Britain–History–Charles I, 1625–1649. 3. Great Britain–
    History–Civil War, 1642–1649. I. Title. II. Series.
    DA405.S38   1999
    941.06–dc21   99–12761
                                    CIP

ISBN 0–415–19902–6

THE ENGLISH WARS AND REPUBLIC,

QUESTIONS AND ANALYSIS IN HISTORY

Edited by Stephen J. Lee and Sean Lang

Other titles in this series:

Imperial Germany, 1871–1918
Stephen J. Lee

The Weimar Republic
Stephen J. Lee

Hitler and Nazi Germany
Stephen J. Lee

Parliamentary Reform, 1785–1928
Sean Lang

The Spanish Civil War
Andrew Forrest

The French Revolution
Jocelyn Hunt

The Renaissance
Jocelyn Hunt

Tudor Government
T. A. Morris

The Cold War
Bradley Lightbody

Stalin and the Soviet Union
Stephen J. Lee

CONTENTS

Illustrations   vi
Series Preface   vii
Acknowledgements   viii

1 The background to the crisis of 1637–1640   1

2 The emergence of Royalists and Roundheads,
  1640–1642   14

3 The war machines, 1642–1646   30

4 The victors fall out and the emergence of
  radicalism, 1646–1649   47

5 The trial and execution of King Charles I and the
  constitutional consequences, 1649–1653   64

6 The Protectorate of Oliver Cromwell, 1653–1658   80

7 Foreign policy during the Protectorate of Oliver
  Cromwell, 1653–1658   99

8 The collapse of the republican experiment,
  1658–1660   109

Notes and sources   122
Select bibliography   133
Index   135

ILLUSTRATIONS

Figure 1   *The Execution of Charles I*, by Weesop   77

Figure 2   Gold crown coin minted during the reign
            of Charles I, 1631–1632   92

Figure 3   Half-crown minted from the period of
            Oliver Cromwell's Protectorate, 1656   92

Figure 4   The royal arms of Stuart   93

Figure 5   The arms of the Protectorate   93

Figure 6   Contemporary Dutch caricature of Oliver
            Cromwell   94

Figure 7   Cromwell crowned by Perfidy and Cruelty:
            a royalist view   95

Figure 8   Oliver Cromwell an engraving by William
            Faithorne the Elder   96

Figure 9   Oliver Cromwell standing in state,
            Somerset House, 1658   97

SERIES PREFACE

Most history textbooks now aim to provide the student with interpretation, and many also cover the historiography of a topic. Some include a selection of sources.

So far, however, there have been few attempts to combine *all* the skills needed by the history student. Interpretation is usually found within an overall narrative framework and it is often difficult to separate out the two for essay purposes. Where sources are included, there is rarely any guidance as to how to answer the questions on them.

The Questions and Analysis series is therefore based on the belief that another approach should be added to those which already exist. It has two main aims.

The first is to separate narrative from interpretation so that the latter is no longer diluted by the former. Most chapters start with a background narrative section containing essential information. This material is then used in a section focusing on analysis through a specific question. The main purpose of this is to help to tighten up essay technique.

The second aim is to provide a comprehensive range of sources for each of the issues covered. The questions are of the type which appear on examination papers, and some have worked answers to demonstrate the techniques required.

The chapters may be approached in different ways. The background narratives can be read first to provide an overall perspective, followed by the analyses and then the sources. The alternative method is to work through all the components of each chapter before going on to the next.

ACKNOWLEDGEMENTS

The author and publishers would like to thank the following for permission to reproduce material:

The Royal Historical Society for extracts from *Proceedings of the Short Parliament of 1640* by H. E. S. Cope and W. H. Coates (eds) (1977); J. M. Dent and Sons for extracts from *Politics, Religion and Literature in the Seventeenth Century* by W. Lamont and S. Oldfield (eds) (1975); John Murray for extracts from *The English Revolution* by B. Coward and C. Durston (eds) (1997); Stanley Thornes for extracts from *People Power and Politics: Was There a Mid-seventeenth Century English Revolution?* by R. Ellis (1992); Cass for extracts from *The Good Old Cause, The English Revolution of 1640–1660* by C. Hill and E. Dell (eds) (1969); Cambridge University Press for extracts from *The English Levellers* by A. Sharp (ed.) (1998), *The Stuart Constitution: Documents and Commentary* by J. P. Kenyon (ed.) (1966), and *Oliver Cromwell: Politics and Religion in the English Revolution, 1640–1658* by David L. Smith (ed.) (1991).

For illustrations used, acknowledgements are due to the following: A & C Black (Publishers) Ltd, *Basic Heraldry* by S. Friar and J. Ferguson (1993); Mansell/Time Inc. Collection; British Museum; Magdalen College, Oxford; the Earl of Rosebery/National Galleries of Scotland and The Fotomas Index (UK) 12 Pickhurst Rise, West Wickham, Kent, BR4 0AL.

While every effort has been made to trace and acknowledge ownership of copyright material used in this volume, the publishers will be glad to make suitable arrangements with any copyright holders whom it has not been possible to contact.

1

THE BACKGROUND TO THE CRISIS OF 1637–1640

BACKGROUND NARRATIVE

Looking back on the 1630s, Lord Falkland was moved to describe that period as 'the most serene, quiet and halcyon days that could possibly be imagined'.[1] At least until 1637 there indeed appears to be little evidence of disaffection towards Caroline government in England. Taxes were paid, laws were enforced and obeyed and there was nothing other than grumbling resentment at Charles's and Archbishop Laud's religious reforms. Yet it was a rather superficial calm, the political nation having been denied a platform from which it might articulate its grievances because of the King's decision – proclaimed on 27 March 1629 after the riotous conclusion to the second session of the 1628 Parliament – not to call any further Parliaments until 'our people shall see more clearly into our intentions and actions'.[2]

Two events in particular suggested that all was not well. First, in June 1637 William Prynne, Henry Burton and John Bastwick were sentenced to be fined, imprisoned and to lose their ears for criticising Laudian innovations, many of which – such as the order that the altar be removed to the east end of churches and railed – smacked of Catholic practices. Second, in October 1637 John Hampden challenged the King's right to levy Ship Money on inland counties without first obtaining the assent of Parliament, a challenge which came close to success when the judges ruled in favour of the King by only seven votes to five.

Neither of these events apparently encouraged other protestations against Caroline government, though recent research has revealed an undercurrent of discontent in England in the 1630s, as recorded in the private diaries of the likes of Simonds D'Ewes. Moreover, unable to accept the Laudian religious programme, significant numbers – perhaps as many as 15,000 – chose to emigrate. Nevertheless, the majority chose to acquiesce, as is indicated most notably in the fact that, until 1639, the majority of demands for Ship Money were paid, prompting Kevin Sharpe to conclude that 'for all its problems [Ship Money] must qualify as one of the most successful taxes . . . in early modern history'.[3]

It is therefore another event of 1637 that is central to any explanation of why Charles called an English Parliament twice in 1640 (the so-called Short and Long Parliaments): the introduction of a new Scottish Prayer Book on 23 July 1637. The Scots regarded this as ecclesiastical imperialism, perceiving the royal action as the beginning of a campaign to bring their Presbyterian Church into line with the Church of England. Public readings of the Prayer Book were thus met with riot and disorder. By February 1638 resistance had crystallised into the form of a National Covenant, a solemn oath that bound the signatories to resist innovation in Church and State. Then, nine months later, exasperated by the actions of Charles, the office of bishop was formally abolished by the Glasgow Assembly.

In other respects the Scots were also challenging Charles's political and constitutional powers in Scotland. For instance, as early as June 1639 Covenanting proposals were being articulated to secure regular Parliaments (every two to three years) and rumour abounded that if the King would not summon them, then the nobility would do so of its own accord. There were also Covenanter demands that the appointments of Privy Councillors, officers of State and officers of the Court of Session were to come under the sphere of parliamentary control, and that those who were perceived as having offered 'evil' advice and were therefore held responsible for the troubles in Scotland – 'incendiaries' such as Laud and Wentworth – should be called to account. A Covenanter programme of this nature had implications for Charles's government of his other kingdoms and therefore had to be resisted.

Thus, in both 1639 and 1640 Charles raised an army in an attempt to coerce the Scots. However, his defeat in these Bishops'

Wars was not only to bring to an end his rule without Parliaments in England but fatally destabilised affairs in his third kingdom, Ireland.

ANALYSIS: WHY DID CHARLES I LOSE THE BISHOPS' WARS?

The First Bishops' War of 1639 developed no further than a military stand-off and resolved nothing. On 4 June, near Kelso, the Scottish commander, Alexander Leslie, Earl of Leven, employing an old trick of the Thirty Years War which involved arranging a herd of cattle behind his army in order to convince the enemy that their opponents possessed a more substantial force than was in fact the case, encouraged the English, under the command of Henry Rich, Earl of Holland, to withdraw. An uneasy truce, the Pacification of Berwick, was consequently signed on 18 June 1639, obliging neither side to make concessions. Ultimately, however, on 28 August 1640 the Scots defeated the English at the Battle of Newburn near Newcastle and thus emerged victorious in the Bishops' Wars, the first time that they had triumphed over their ancient enemy since Bannockburn in 1314. Clarendon recorded his belief that the rout amounted to the 'most shameful and confounding flight that was ever heard of'.[4] The prospect of fighting fellow Protestants at the very time that rumours of a Popish Plot abounded seems to have sapped the fighting fervour of the English. Nevertheless, defeat was also a result of the fact that England was fundamentally incapable of waging effective war against her northern neighbour in 1639 and 1640 (for reasons that historians have been unable to ascertain indisputably). Was this a circumstance brought about by the deficiencies of antiquated institutions and systems, particularly that by which local government operated, or was it begotten by the shortcomings of individuals, most especially those of the King himself?

As a British king, Charles I resolved upon using the resources of two of his kingdoms, Ireland and England, in order to bring the third, Scotland, to heel. On paper this appeared a sound, realistic policy whereas in actuality it was overambitious and ill-constructed. Thus, three of the four aspects of the strategy devised for 1639 failed to materialise. First, the seaborne invasion force commanded by the Duke of Hamilton – one of the King's closest advisers on Scottish affairs – did not land at Aberdeen, at least partly because Charles had failed to exploit divisions within the Covenanters and thereby win a royal party in Scotland. Thereafter, the fleet proved ineffective when blockading Edinburgh. Second, the promised attack upon the west coast of Scotland from Ireland by Randal MacDonnell, Earl of Antrim – a leading Irish Catholic who possessed extensive lands in northern Ireland and claimed as inheritance holdings in western Scotland that lay under control of the Campbells, the clan leader of whom was the Archibald Campbell, Earl of Argyll – never manifested itself, though the mere threat had been sufficient to force the powerful Argyll into the ranks of the Covenanters and thus enhanced the wherewithal of the Scots to withstand the royal will. Third, the Irish expeditionary force of perhaps 10,000 men commanded by Thomas Wentworth, Earl of Strafford – a leading exponent of the Personal Rule and Lord Deputy of Ireland from 1632 – never made it to Dumbarton. Nevertheless, when Charles set about devising the campaign for 1640 Strafford reminded him that he had an army in Ireland that 'you may employ here to reduce this kingdom', though it proved impossible to mobilise this force in time to thwart the Scots at Newburn.[5] Yet even if this force had arrived, since it was largely composed of Catholics – though most of the officers were Protestant – it would probably have inflamed the Scots and stiffened their resistance. The only force that the King successfully mobilised and led in both 1639 and 1640 was an English army numbering between 15,000 and 20,000, probably the rough equivalent of the Covenanting forces under the leadership of Alexander Leslie. However, stubbornly refusing to accept advice except from those who told him what he wanted to hear, Charles wrongly assumed that on both occasions money, supplies and men would be available at a few months' notice.

Although substantial English armies were mobilised in 1639 and 1640, they were significantly composed of raw, ill-disciplined, 'beggarly fellows'. 'Our soldiers are so disorderly that they shoot bullets through our tents,' recorded one officer.[6] Despite an attempt to do so in the early 1630s, Charles had not created a 'perfect militia' – county forces that were well equipped and mustered regularly for training. More damaging still to the King's military effort was his decision to allow militiamen to avoid service according to the substitution clause, a device that allowed them to hire a replacement – invariably an untrained fellow from the lower orders of society. As Mark C. Fissel has observed, 'the wholescale exploitation of that loophole, especially in 1640, produced an army quite different from that which had been planned' and it is thus a major factor in explaining the defeat at Newburn.[7] Untrained replacements for the militia, along with men who had been pressed, probably made up one half of the English forces in 1639 and 1640. 'I daresay', noted Sir Edmund Verney, 'there was never so raw, so unskilful and so unwilling an army brought to fight.'[8]

Little wonder that this army of 1640 became ' the greatest law enforcement problem in living memory'.[9]

A dearth of serviceable weapons further lessened the prospect for successful royal campaigns. One consequence of England's long years of peace was that new weapons were not easily to be had. Many of the musket makers, for example, had emigrated to the Netherlands where they had a ready market in the warring factions in the Thirty Years War. Although 2,000 pikes were ordered from the Netherlands, none was efficient. Thus, in 1639 the Kentish men had to make do with 'muskets having not tough holes' and 'pikes . . . so rotten as they were shaken . . . all to pieces'.[10] As Conrad Russell has observed: ' . . . the lack of arms clearly contributed to the lack of fighting spirit amongst the English troops'.[11] This was a problem that grew yet worse in 1640. Just ten days before the Battle of Newburn Francis Windebank reported to his father that his troops had no arms with which to fight. The following day, Asburnham told Nicholas that more than one-third of the army remained unarmed. In 1640 the Privy Council was informed by the armourers that they could produce arms for 700 foot each month, according to which rate an English army of 30,000 would be replete with arms in three and a half years!

The condition of the troops was not improved by the leadership under which they laboured. Thomas Howard, Earl of Arundel, appointed Lord General in 1639, was a figure whom Clarendon considered 'had nothing martial about him but his presence and his looks'.[12] He was replaced in 1640 by the much more suitable Algernon Percy, Earl of Northumberland, but he, like Strafford, was immobilised by illness in August of that year and could not take the field thereafter. Unable to afford the hire of mercenaries, most of Charles I's commanders were lords, knights and gentlemen who had never experienced battle. Of those who gained much-needed experience in 1639, many were replaced for the campaign of the following summer on the orders of Charles. Meanwhile, keen to support their King in what was seen as a religious war, a significant number of Catholics served as officers only to induce suspicion and hostility among the troops. Two such officers were murdered by soldiers in 1640.

The effectiveness of the English forces was also severely diminished because of a lack of funds. By choosing to mobilise an army in 1639 without calling a Parliament, and then mobilising another force in the following year despite the fact that the Short Parliament of 1640 was addled (producing no legislation or subsidies), Charles was obliged to rely upon the fiscal devices of the Crown prerogative. Yet it was unrealistic to expect these means alone to provide sufficient money to wage war successfully. Indeed, throughout the 1630s yearly expenditures had approximated to revenues. There was thus no brimming war chest at Westminster. Moreover, the 'dead marketts' and dearth of trade that afflicted England meant that loans were difficult to raise. 'Money is very scarce and hard to be gotten,' remarked one contemporary.[13] In December 1639, echoing concerns that had been voiced about the previous campaign, Northumberland lamented that 'a mighty army is intended for the north, but no man knows how it will be paid'.[14]

Lack of money meant that a large army could not easily be kept in the field because of growing ill-discipline and an increasing propensity to mutiny. Thus, despite the fact that he had a sizeable army in the field and the ostensible support of the greater part of the political nation in 1639, Charles opened negotiations with the Covenanters – an event that John Adamson considers to have been 'arguably the greatest single mistake of Charles I's life'.[15] Moreover, the Second Bishops' War appears to have been lost before the bulk of the army had reached the battlefield because the government, realising that the troops remained a charge on the counties rather than the Exchequer until they crossed the county boundaries, fatally postponed the general rendezvous from 1 June until July, thus allowing the Covenanters to invade with extraordinary ease.

A widespread anger at what many perceived to be Charles I's lack of respect for the law sapped many Englishmen's resolve to fight for their King. Indeed, Russell believes that this 'made a significant contribution to English failure in the Second Bishops' War, and perhaps in the First also'.[16] The military prerogative of the Crown had already come under attack in the Parliament of 1628, in particular when the Crown's alleged right to impress men suffered a damaging legal challenge. Moreover, since the Act permitting the Crown to demand the services of the militia – a form of citizenry in arms organised on a county basis and controlled by the Lords Lieutenant – had been allowed to lapse in 1604, there was now no legal basis left for the militia except for the prerogative. The fact that the King allowed Convocation – the assembly of the clergy – to continue to sit beyond the dissolution of the Short Parliament was also legally questionable, Convocation usually terminating at the same time as Parliament.

Charles also created suspicion and concern as to what his real intentions were because of his obvious reluctance to call Parliament, the only forum in which members of the political nation could air their grievances in the hope that they would be redressed by the Crown. When Charles mobilised his forces in 1639 it was the first time that the

Crown had attempted to wage war without the support of Parliament since 1323. It was a decision that weakened the royal offensive, not least because thereafter Lords Brooke and Saye and Sele refused to take an oath on the basis that it was not validated by Parliament, thus encouraging others to resist by their actions. Ultimately persuaded by Strafford to meet with a Parliament in the spring of 1640, Charles showed himself to be dangerously out of sympathy with members of both Houses by insisting that they should 'lay aside all other debates' in preference to passing subsidies.

Returning to their counties without royal concessions, MPs, who were also key members of local government, found it increasingly difficult to force payment of various taxes and compel obedience to the royal will in the localities. When John Pym, in a widely reported speech, informed his listeners in the Short Parliament that military charges were being levied 'without ground or law' resistance became much more pervasive.[17] Indeed, local government now witnessed a form of functional breakdown. Deputy lieutenants and constables – those responsible for raising and training the militia and collecting levies such as coat and conduct money – were prepared to provide their (unpaid) services only for as long as the work advanced their standing with their neighbours. However, increasingly such work made men 'ill saviour' to their countrymen. In Somerset, for instance, local officials confessed that they had become more frightened of their neighbours than the Crown. It is not surprising that in 1639–1640 there occurred a taxpayers' strike. 'So general a disaffection in this kingdom hath not been known in the memory of any,' wrote Northumberland in 1640.[18]

Perhaps most damaging to the royal war effort was the fact that Charles had assumed that traditional English hatred of the Scots remained greater than English hatred of the Personal Rule. In truth, an increasing number of English – egged on by a Scottish propaganda campaign that warned 'when we're slain, the rod comes to your breech' (see Source B) – were coming to sympathise with the Scots.[19] 'Your grievances are ours,' declared a Scottish leaflet that was circulating in Essex. 'The preservation of religion and liberties is common to both nations: we must now stand or fall together.'[20] To many of the English, the Scots were no longer seen as the enemy, but as liberators. Hamilton had recorded his belief as early as 1638 that this would diminish the spirit of the English to fight, that they 'will not be so forward in this as they ought'.[21] Recent research has demonstrated that passive sympathy became positive collusion, the first time since 1216 that a significant body of Englishmen had allied with an invading army against their own king, colluding with and advising the royal opposition. Indeed, on the same day that the Scots invaded England, Charles faced concerted opposition from twelve leading peers beseeching 'your most Excellent Majesty that he would be pleased to summon a Parliament'.[22] It seems clear that Charles was obliged to fight both Bishops' Wars with a fifth column at his rear, a circumstance that fatally diminished the efficacy of the English war machine.

Effective strategy, efficient officers, trained soldiers, ample supply, strong leadership and, indeed, luck are all necessary in order to enjoy success in war. Yet in each respect the royal campaigns of the Bishops' Wars were deficient. It is true that Charles was obliged to rely upon outdated institutions but by and large they seem to have worked as well as could have been expected – after all, two sizeable armies were raised. This is especially remarkable since royal actions not only eroded the willingness of members of the gentry and merchant classes to assist the Crown but rendered local government practically inoperable. It seems that in the Bishops' Wars Charles I was his own worst enemy.

Questions

1. 'In 1640 Charles was defeated less by the Scots and more by the inefficiencies of the institutions with which he had to work'. Discuss
2. Could Charles have avoided defeat in the Bishops' Wars?

SOURCES

1. ENGLISH DEFEAT IN THE SECOND BISHOPS' WAR

Source A: Windebanke to Conway, Deputy General of the British Army, 7 May 1640.

[The Scots] have too much encouragement by the unhappy rupture of the parliament who have clearly discovered they like their courses so well that they would contribute nothing towards their suppression.

Source B: from the pen of a Scottish balladeer at the time of the Bishops' Wars, written for an English audience.

What will you fight, for a Book of Common Prayer?
What will you fight, for a Court of High Commission?

What will you fight, for a mitre gilded fair?
Or to maintain the prelates proud ambition?
What will you get? Your yoke will be lighter
For when we're slain, the rod comes to your breech.

Source C: Strafford to Hamilton, 24 August 1640.

I am not sorry the Scots are come in . . . certainly it will give his Majesty many great advantages which might have been disputed had we been the aggressors.

Source D: Northumberland to Leicester, 18 June 1640.

I know not what to think of our army. The men that are pressed run so fast away and are so mutinous that I doubt we shall want [lack] a very great part of our number; and those that remain will be readier to draw their swords upon their officers than against the Scots.

Source E: Sir Edward Osborne at York, 1640.

I doubt extremely our forces are not now in so ready a condition as they were last year, very many arms being lost in that expedition and none to be bought ever since for supply of defects.

Source F: G. Burnet, 1677.

No sooner did the Scottish cannon begin to play but they [the English], struck with fear, threw down their arms and ran away.

Source G: extract from a letter written by Conway.

Now, upon the whole matter it may easily be judged whether the two actions of the retreat at Newburn and quitting Newcastle were the causes of our losses, or the effects of ill-grounded designs: to make a war without means, to go on with it, and to begin it at sea thereby giving the Scots a pretext to attempt us by land before we were able to resist them.

Questions

1. (i) Explain the reference in Source A to 'the unhappy rupture of Parliament'.
    (ii) Explain the reference in Source E to arms lost in 'that expedition'. [4]
2. Compare and explain the opinions given in Sources C and G as to whether it was England or Scotland which possessed the initial advantage in the Second Bishops' War. [5]

*3. Read Source B. In what ways would a historian researching reasons for the English defeat in the Second Bishops' War find this a useful source? [4]

4. With reference to both its content and provenance, assess the reliability of Source D. [4]

5. Use these sources and your own knowledge to explain why the English forces were defeated at the Battle of Newburn. [8]

Worked answer

*3. The historian would infer that Scottish opinion believed that the King's motives for fighting were of a religious nature – for the preservation of the Book of Common Prayer and the retention of High Commission and episcopacy. Moreover, since the writer is attempting to persuade the English not to fight – informing the English that 'when we're slain, the rod comes to your breech' – it is clear that Scottish opinion believed that the English were disaffected towards these ecclesiastical aspects of Charles I's government. Above all, this source is useful to the historian because it is an example of Scottish propaganda and an indication of how the Covenanters disabled the English war effort.

SOURCES

2. THE SHORT PARLIAMENT, 13 APRIL–5 MAY 1640

Source H: Sir Benjamin Rudyerd's speech to the Commons, 16 April 1640.

Heretofore the distempers of the House have been imputed to the papists but the happy success of this Parliament seems to be [in] the general power of all . . . Therefore it is wisdom in us to preserve [use] moderation and caution. Breakings of Parliaments makes dangerous wounds in the body politique and if these splinters be not pulled out with a gentle hand we may hereafter despair of cure . . . A Parliament is the bed of reconciliation betwixt king and people and therefore it is fit for us to lay aside all exasperations and carry ourselves with humility howbeit the King's Prerogative may go far . . . Princes are and will be as jealous of their power as people of their liberties, though both are best when kept within their bounds. Levying of moneys are a great disturbance to the subjects, and so will the scarcity of the King's revenues until they be supplied, and where the power and necessity meet in one hand he will not be disappointed.

Source I: extracts from Sir Francis Seymour's speech to the Commons, 16 April 1640.

His Majesty I believe hath as great affection to parliaments as ever ... but we must not do him a disservice in neglecting the Commonwealth ... for if we should grant the King subsidies before our grievances are debated and redressed our judgements may very well be questioned, and it may give the country (whom we serve) cause to blame the men whom they have chosen as consenting to their sufferance and it may likewise be taken as a confirmation of our grievances ... His Majesty is the sun, which though it always shines alike in itself Gloriously, yet by reason of clouds it may not so appear. If Majesty by the reason of bad members appears not in such splendour, what will it avail us if the fountain be clear, if the streams that issue therefrom be not so also, so though the King be never so just, his bad ministers may corrupt his justice.

Source J: from the recorded proceedings of the Lords and Commons in the Short Parliament.

Lower House – 2 May
The King sends to the House to grant him moneys without delay, and that he would have 12 subsidies. The House sits all day debating what to do. [The] King offered that if the House would give him 12 subsidies for his [present] necessity then he would take off the Ship Money.

Lower House – 5 May
The House consulted what to do and what answer to give. It was feared [anticipated] that they would have yielded to have given 6 subsidies but before it came to voting the King breaks up the House as being unwilling to have that dishonour, that the Parliament should vote against him.

Source K: extract from the 23rd article of impeachment against Strafford, 28 January 1641.

... and while the said Commons [in the Short Parliament] then assembled, ... Strafford ... did procure his Majesty to dissolve the said Parliament upon the fifth day of May last, and upon the same day ... did treacherously, falsely and maliciously endeavour to incense his Majesty against his loving and faithful subjects ... by telling his Majesty they [MPs] had denied to supply him. And afterwards upon the same day he did traitorously and wickedly counsel and advise his Majesty to this effect; viz., that having tried the affections of his people, he was loosed and absolved from all rules of government ... and that he had an army in Ireland ... which he might employ to reduce this kingdom.

Source L: proceedings of the Short Parliament, 5 May 1640.

This day the King came and both Houses assembled. His Majesty gave the Lords thanks and promised that out of Parliament as well as in he would preserve the unity of the Religion in the Church of England, and the propriety of goods, and liberties of his people. But for the cunning and ill affection of many in the Lower House, [whose delays were] worse than denial, he commanded the Keeper to dissolve the Parliament which he did.

Questions

1. (i) Explain the reference to 'papists' in Source H. [1]
   (ii) What might you infer from Source L were the actual 'distempers' (Source H) and 'grievances' (Source I) of MPs in the Short Parliament? [3]
2. Read Source I. Which other source in this collection best supports Seymour's opinion? Explain your choice. [2]
*3. Read Sources H and I. With reference to tone and language, compare the effectiveness of these two speeches. [6]
4. How useful is Source J for a historian researching the reign of Charles I? [4]
5. Use these sources and your own knowledge to explain the failure of the Short Parliament. [10]

Worked answer

*3. Considering the general atmosphere that prevailed in the Short Parliament, many MPs are likely to have resented the speech made by Rudyerd. His tone is one of caution and of acquiescence. For example, he suggests that in order to enjoy a 'happy success' MPs should proceed with 'moderation'. This, he says, would be an act of 'wisdom'. Moreover, he asserts that MPs should 'lay aside all exasperations' and display 'humility', even if the 'King's Prerogative may go far'. He endeavours to win support by employing a rather ill-conceived simile, describing all that is wrong as a 'splinter' and yet alleging that these make 'dangerous wounds'.

Seymour also employs similes in his speech. However – unlike Rudyerd's – these are accessible and vivid, his references to the 'sun', 'clouds', 'streams' and 'fountain' serving to bring colour to the argument that though 'His Majesty . . . hath as great affection to parliaments as ever' his good intentions are ill served by 'bad ministers'. Not only is Seymour's tone much less cautious than that of Rudyerd – he even suggests that no subsidies should be given 'before our grievances are debated' – but the manner in which he justifies his position appears entirely convincing. Thus, Seymour argues that MPs would actually be doing the King a 'disservice' if they immediately provided him with subsidies. In any case, until 'the fountain be clear' there was every reason not to supply royal needs.

For these reasons, and considering the nature of the audience, Source I is the more effective.

2

THE EMERGENCE OF ROYALISTS AND ROUNDHEADS, 1640–1642

BACKGROUND NARRATIVE

After the Long Parliament first met on 3 November 1640 MPs set about removing what they regarded as the abuses and abusers of the Personal Rule. The abolition of Crown devices like High Commission and Ship Money and the dismissal of royal servants such as Laud and Strafford was done in the expectation that their removal would lead automatically to an improvement in the body politic. However, no such improvement occurred. Instead, the King himself was implicated in a number of schemes that envisaged the use of force against Crown opponents: the first and second Army Plots, the 'Incident' and the Antrim Plot.

The first Army Plot, revealed by Pym to the Commons on 3 May 1641, was a scheme whereby a group of army officers was to capture the Tower, release Strafford and threaten Parliament with dissolution. When this design failed to materialise a similar scheme (even though Strafford had been executed on 12 May 1641) seems to have been devised in June, though Pym, determined to use the machinations of Charles to his own advantage, chose to reveal the existence of the second Army Plot as late as 30 October. Meanwhile, on 11–12 October Charles had conspired in the so-called 'Incident', a botched attempt to arrest Argyll, the leading Covenanter, and Hamilton, whom the King had come to suspect as guilty of treason. Historians are unable to agree upon whether Charles was conspiring over the summer and autumn of 1641 with the Earl of Antrim in order to mobilise Irish Catholic troops, but the fact that the Irish rebels of October 1641, led by Sir Phelim O'Neill, claimed that Charles had sent them a commission authorising them to take up arms certainly makes the King appear guilty of such a course of action.

Thus, when the Irish rebellion occurred in October 1641 the reforming element in Parliament, driven forward by John Pym and his supporters in the Lords, concluded that a duplicitous king could not be trusted at the head of an army raised by Parliament. The extent to which it was feasible to invade the Crown prerogative rather than restrain it now moved to the top of the political agenda and proved highly divisive; the Grand Remonstrance, a document demanding further concessions of the royal prerogative, passed in the Commons by only eleven votes on 22 November 1641. Polarisation of allegiances among members of the English political nation became yet more extreme because of Parliament's campaign to abolish episcopacy 'root and branch', a demand induced by pressure from the Scots, victors over the King in the Second Bishops' War and facilitators of the calling of the Long Parliament.

ANALYSIS (1): 'IN NOVEMBER 1640 AN ENGLISH CIVIL WAR WAS UNLIKELY; BY JANUARY 1642 IT WAS BOTH POSSIBLE AND PROBABLE.' TO WHAT EXTENT DO YOU AGREE WITH THIS STATEMENT?

It is no longer possible to accept the notion that Crown and Parliament had been on a collision course for several decades before 1642: a Whiggish interpretation of events that has been discredited by revisionist historians – though they in turn have been criticised by the post-revisionists for placing an undue emphasis upon those elements in early Stuart political culture that stressed order, harmony and consensus.[1] Similarly, despite the claims of some Marxist historians, it is equally difficult to argue that social and economic developments created circumstances in which civil war became unavoidable. After all, England suffered no major rebellion beyond the middle of the sixteenth century, no peer was tried for treason during the years 1601–1639 and, unlike the rest of Europe, tax collectors needed no royal protection. Moreover, from the 1570s the incidence of riot declined decade by decade. Historians have therefore sought the origins of the Civil War in the period immediately prior to its outbreak, most especially in the years 1637–1642. Recent research has further suggested that the English Civil War may properly be understood only by viewing events from their British perspective. Observing that Scotland and Ireland rebelled before England, Conrad Russell has articulated a three-kingdom 'billiard ball' explanation for the outbreak of conflict in England.[2] However, Russell's argument that rebellions in Scotland and Ireland were necessary preconditions for the same process in England has met with criticism. John Morrill, for example, believes that 'at times Russell seems to let the Scottish tail wag the English dog' and that, at least in religious matters, since 'there was by 1640 a "coiled spring" of godly zeal' in England, rebellion in that nation was not necessarily dependent upon Scottish actions.[3]

The essential precondition for a civil war was absent in England in 1640: two 'sides' did not exist. The King did not command the support of a 'party' whose resources he might employ to fight his opponents, a result of the royal decision to rule without calling a Parliament for eleven years (1629–1640) and Charles choosing instead to govern by relying upon other aspects of the Crown prerogative. Thus, by 1640 the greater part of the political nation was united against Caroline government. However, after the Long Parliament first met in November 1640 there began to emerge a royal 'party'.

This surge of support for Charles came about because an increasingly large number of MPs became suspicious of the objectives of John Pym and his supporters, or Junto. Many became concerned that the due processes of law were being ignored when it was resolved to attaint Strafford, a legislative procedure that simply enacted that the Lord Deputy was guilty of treason and thus deprived him of a right to defend himself. It is instructive that the decision to attaint Strafford on 21 April 1641 took place in a Commons in which little more than half the House was present. Lord Digby lamented that they were 'committing murder with the sword of justice'.[4] Even more divisive was Pym's demand that Parliament acquire some influence over the appointment of Crown ministers, a consistent aspect of the Junto's policy since it had first been mooted in the Ten Propositions of 24 June 1641.[5] By the end of the year Pym was insisting that Parliament would not help Charles suppress the Irish rebellion unless he conceded to them the right to nominate royal councillors, a central theme of both the

Additional Instruction of 8 November and the Grand Remonstrance.[6] Yet many MPs baulked at such an invasion of the Crown prerogative. Swords were drawn during the debate on the Grand Remonstrance, a document that eventually passed the House on 22 November by only 159 votes to 148. Nor was it only what the Remonstrance contained that caused disaffection, but the fact that it was designed as an appeal to the people. Edward Dering articulated the fears of many when he remarked that he 'did not dream that we should remonstrate downward, tell stories to the people and talk of the King as of a third person'.[7]

Recent research has suggested that those who became activists in the period 1641–1642 were most keenly agitated by religion. Those men who had a long-standing commitment to a strict Calvinist theology and to further reformation of the Church – those who sought to abolish episcopacy 'root and branch' – were also the men who pushed the Houses into taking a tougher stand against the King. For them, this was the moment when the Reformation begun in the sixteenth century could be finally concluded. If the King would not give his assent to this process then he would have to be coerced.

It is less easy to single out a religious motive when analysing those who became Royalists. It is certainly true that the majority of Royalists wished to preserve the existing structures and practices of the Church of England but they also sided with the King because they feared that the abolition of bishops would lead to a general breakdown in law and order and, moreover, resented the way in which 'King Pym' appeared determined to usurp the established prerogative of the Crown. From these circumstances there emerged the constitutional royalists – men like Edward Hyde, Viscount Falkland and Sir John Culpepper. Amongst other things, they believed that the Church of England should be preserved from 'root and branch' reform and 'that Charles I could be trusted to rule legally and to abide by the safeguards erected in 1640–1'.[8]

Yet it was also as a result of his own actions, and not just the negative effect of the machinations of Pym and his Junto, that Charles earned himself a 'party'. For instance, he assented to the abolition of all the key features of the Personal Rule. Not only did Ship Money and the prerogative courts of Star Chamber and High Commission now disappear but so too did the 'incendiaries' of the 1630s such as Laud and Strafford, the former imprisoned in the Tower (until his execution on 10 January 1645) whilst the latter was executed on 12 May 1641. Meanwhile, according to the terms of the Triennial Act of 16 February 1641, Charles was henceforth obliged to call a Parliament at least once every three years. Moreover, as a result of Charles having given his assent to a Bill on 10 May 1641, he could not dissolve the present Parliament without its own consent. To a growing number of the political nation, Charles therefore appeared to be offering what he had promised in a speech on 25 January 1641 – 'reformation rather than alteration', an increasingly appealing scenario in the face of the growing disorder and unquiet that seemed to be the consequence of Pym's actions.[9] Furthermore, to counter accusations that he was caught up in a plot to return England to Rome, Charles exhibited his adherence to Protestantism by marrying his daughter, Mary, to the Protestant William of Orange on 2 May 1641. Finally, the King won yet more favour by promoting several bishops and appointing new ones, all of whom were opponents of Laud. In particular, John Williams was made Archbishop of York despite the fact that he had spent 1637–1640 in the Tower as a result of his anti-Laudian activities.

Yet the formation of sides meant only that conflict became possible, not that it is was necessarily probable. After all, whenever differences exist between parties there is always a possibility that they will either be resolved or reduced in their significance by negotiation and compromise. Why was there no settlement in 1641? Part of the answer is that by his own actions Charles provided Pym and his Junto with reason to believe that the concessions he had already made were insincere. By allowing himself to be implicated in a series of schemes such as the first and second Army Plots and the 'Incident' – all of which were intent upon using force against the English and Scottish Parliaments – Charles betrayed the notion that he intended his concessions to be short-lived. He had a remarkable ability for effecting ill-timed, ill-advised actions. For instance, his appointment of Thomas Lunsford as Lieutenant of the Tower, 'a young outlaw' and 'swaggering ruffian' who had been pardoned for an alleged murder attempt, enhanced misgivings about the King's real intentions.[10] As a result of such actions Pym and his Junto were thus obliged to become more extreme in their demands, a process that historians have chosen to call 'functional radicalism'. It follows that the chances of a settlement lessened as their demands became more extreme.

The prospects for a settlement were made even less likely because of the presence of the Scots in English political affairs. The consequences of the Scottish invasion of England in August 1640 had created conditions in which Parliament was again called in November of that year. The combined effect of the Treaty of Ripon – which stipulated that Charles pay £850 per day to the Scots or face renewed hostilities – and the fact that the Commons deprived Charles of control of some 60 per cent of his ordinary revenues during 1641 prevented Charles from dissolving Parliament and by so doing depriving his opponents of their campaign platform. Therefore, since Pym and his Junto owed their position to the Scots it was absolutely necessary to their self-preservation that they keep the support of their northern neighbours. The most effective way to do this was by implementing some of the war aims of the Covenanters, especially those designed to emasculate Charles's authority in England; in particular the abolition of bishops.

The Scots were understandably fearful that at some point in the future Charles would be able to gain sufficient support to mobilise the greater resources of his southern kingdom in order to dismantle the Covenanting revolution in Scotland which, among other things, was represented by the formal abolition of episcopacy, the acquisition by the Scottish Parliament of the right of nomination of judicial and executive appointments, the calling of triennial Parliaments and, whilst Parliament was not in session, committees of MPs sitting during the interval. Henceforth, it was central to the Covenanting cause that episcopacy be abolished in Charles's southern kingdom, not only because episcopacy was hated by the Covenanters for genuine religious and doctrinal reasons, but because the bishops would be central to any mobilisation of English resources.

On this point Charles was as immovable as had been his father: 'No bishop, no King.'[11] Possessed of such an attitude, there was no ground for compromise. Charles could not consent to the bishops in England becoming 'no better than cyphers'.[12] More generally, as a British king he could not contemplate the abolition of episcopacy in one of his kingdoms. British affairs in this way thwarted a negotiated settlement. Charles could no more relinquish bishops than Pym's group could relinquish the Scots.

The chances of a settlement were at their greatest in the spring of 1641 when the Earl of Bedford, Pym's patron in the Lords, was at the centre of a scheme that would have offered Charles a meaningful financial settlement in exchange for his agreeing to nominate to important positions of government leading critics of the Crown among peers and MPs. However, the scheme died along with Bedford on 9 May 1641, an event that 'is believed by some historians to have destroyed any possibility of a lasting compromise between Charles I and the controlling figures in the two Houses'.[13] Even if Bedford had survived, it seems probable that Scottish pressure would have prevented implementation of the plan. This was because the Scots were intent upon the removal of Strafford (the architect of the Second Bishops'

War). However, as Anthony Fletcher has pointed out, 'the King's attitude to the plan for bridge appointments rested on Parliament's willingness to spare Strafford's life', which they were not prepared to countenance.[14] Moreover, because the Scottish demands increasingly aroused resentment in England, this in turn served to encourage support for Charles. 'The Royalist party was an anti-Scottish party before it was a Royalist party,' observes Russell.[15] With his 'party' growing in number, Charles was less inclined to negotiate.

The presence of two parties and the absence of a negotiated settlement meant that a resort to force was increasingly likely, though by this stage it was not inevitable. In September 1641, with at least some of their demands having been met and formalised in the Treaty of London, the Covenanting occupation force went back to Scotland and in so doing significantly reduced the political clout of Pym's Junto. If Charles had now prorogued Parliament (that is, suspended the session), he could yet have dissipated the opposition. However, having travelled to Scotland to sign the Treaty of London, the King chose to linger there and missed this opportunity. Furthermore, the outbreak of the Irish rebellion in October 1641 ensured that any such chance would not recur in the near future. This was because it was now necessary for Charles to keep Parliament sitting in order that it might provide supplies to furnish an army against the Irish insurrection, thus effectively 'handcuffing' together both 'sides' at the very time when relations between them were tense and embittered. At the same time, the Irish rebellion posed with acute urgency the question of the King's military authority: the issue over which King and Parliament were to go to war in 1642. In this way events in Ireland induced an even greater polarisation of opinion among members of the English political nation and led to a hardening of their respective positions.

Predictably, many MPs refused to contemplate allowing Charles his established prerogative power to head any army that they funded precisely because he had given them sufficient reason to fear that he might employ the very same army upon themselves. Therefore, there were only two ways in which the handcuffs might yet be removed. The first was for one 'side' to attract sufficient support from the other so that, lacking a 'party', the latter element would have to accept some sort of dictated settlement. The second was for providing vital leadership in either camp to be removed so that the effectiveness of that camp would be diminished. Pym tried, and failed, to achieve the former of these by appealing to the people in the form of the Grand Remonstrance. Charles, on the other hand – in an act that demonstrated his belief that events were driven forward by only a few 'malignants' – attempted to arrest those he perceived as orchestrators of the opposition: John Pym, William Strode, Sir Arthur Haselrige, John Hampden, Denzil Holles and Lord Kimbolton. If, indeed, these men had been guilty of colluding with the Scots, then Charles had a very strong legal basis on which he might move against them. However, without explaining the reasons for his action, the King descended upon the Commons in person on 4 January 1642, accompanied by a number of musketeers, only to realise that 'the birds had flown'. By his action, Charles was guilty of breaching an established privilege of Parliament – that MPs should be free from arrest during parliamentary sessions – and thus seemed to confirm opposition MPs' fears that the King could not be trusted. Moreover, the failure of Charles's attempt to arrest the named MPs closed the final exit route from the crisis. As a consequence, after January 1642 the outbreak of an English civil war seemed not only possible but highly probable.

The formation of sides, the absence of a negotiated settlement and the appearance of a particular issue over which to fight are prerequisites for any conflict. Ominously, all were present in the English political system by the end of 1641.

Questions

1. To what extent do events from April 1640 to November 1641 suggest that civil war could have been avoided?
2. At what point did an English civil war become inevitable?

ANALYSIS (2): HOW APPROPRIATE IS JOHN PYM'S EPITHET, 'KING PYM'? WHAT WERE HIS OBJECTIVES AND BY WHAT MEANS DID HE ATTEMPT TO REALISE THEM IN THE PERIOD APRIL 1640–JANUARY 1642?

By the autumn of 1641, very probably as a result of his chairmanship of the Recess Committee, Pym was beginning to be referred to by his critics as 'King Pym'. However, historians have been unable to agree upon the extent of Pym's influence in the early 1640s. On the one hand, Conrad Russell has argued that Pym should be regarded as the single most important figure in the Commons until the outbreak of the English Civil War in 1642, a notion that is supported by both Clarendon's conclusion that Pym was 'the most able to do hurt' and the Venetian ambassador's assertion that he was the 'director of the whole machine'.[16] On the other hand, the notion that Pym was the prime mover of events has met with criticism. John Adamson has suggested that men of business in the Commons were simply doing the bidding of 'opposition' elements in the Lords, that Pym's 'king-makers were members of the House of Lords'.[17] Sheila Lambert has gone yet further and argued for 'the myth of Pym's leadership'.[18] In John Morrill's words, 'she has shown that it is wrong to see Pym as a parliamentary jack of all trades who could and did turn his hand to whatever the occasion demanded'. Morrill himself has argued a case for Pym being simply the most *visible* figure in the Commons at this time.[19] Nevertheless, at key moments during the period 1640–1642 Pym does appear to have been central to the course of events, perhaps even a 'political engineer'.[20]

The objectives of Pym are best identified by examining his great set-piece speeches, most especially those given at the beginnings of the Short and Long Parliaments. During the former he summarised the 'grievances which afflict the Commonwealth'. He told his listeners that there were concerns as to the 'liberties and privileges of Parliament', 'innovations in matters of religion' and the 'propriety of our goods'. He lamented as a 'great grievance' the 'divers innovations in religion' and articulated the notion that there existed a scheme to effect a 'union between us and Rome', a Popish Plot. This was, he said, a result of the damage done by 'the interval of parliaments' because 'where the intercourse of the spirits betwixt the head and the members is hindered the body prospers not'. This decay of the body politic had come about not because of the poor statesmanship of Charles I but because the Privy Councillors were no longer 'Lights of the Realm'. It therefore followed that once the King had been deprived of his evil councillors a political settlement would be able to proceed between, on the one hand, those members of the English political nation disaffected by the Personal Rule and, on the other hand, the Crown. By November 1640 it was a matter of some urgency that this should occur, that the 'design to alter the kingdom both in religion and government' be duly thwarted.[21]

By the time Parliament began its six-week recess on 9 September 1641 Pym's achievement was already substantial. Not only had the prerogative courts of High Commission and Star Chamber been abolished but the judicial powers of the Privy Council, the Council in the North and the Council in the Marches had been suppressed, tonnage and poundage had been abolished, Ship Money and Knighthood fines had been declared illegal and the evil councillors had fled, been impeached or executed. Finally, the King had also assented to the Triennial Bill on 16 February 1641, the terms of which obliged the monarch henceforth to meet with a Parliament for at least fifty days every three years. Many of the grievances of the political nation had been redressed. How was this achieved?

Accumulated grievances could only be redressed through the platform provided by a Parliament. Thus – particularly having experienced the dissolution of the Short Parliament on 5 May 1640 after only three weeks – it was essential to Pym's purpose that he find some means of sustaining the Parliament that first met in November of that year. To the fulfilment of this end he appears to have colluded with the Scots, encouraging them to invade England in the Second Bishops' War. The ensuing armistice (the Treaty of Ripon) demanded a payment of £850 per day from the bankrupt Charles I. Thus, in the expectation that it would provide him with subsidies, Charles I was in this way obliged to call a Parliament. Meanwhile, from Pym's point of view, for as long as there was a Scottish occupation force in the north of England the prerogative of the Crown was compromised. Henry Marten even argued 'for the Scotch army to stay here, and rather to disband our own army'.[22] As a result, unable either to prorogue or dissolve Parliament peremptorily, the King would be obliged to offer concessions in return for subsidies.

It was therefore in the interests of Pym to ensure that the final terms of a peace treaty (the eventual Treaty of London) between the Scots and the King took as long as possible to resolve. One way of achieving this end was by giving priority to those issues pertinent to the English side of a settlement with Charles. According to Russell, by 'taking refuge in the area where inaction, rather than action, could achieve their objectives, Pym and his parliamentary junto were playing their cards with considerable skill'.[23] Pym further bolstered his position by reaffirming the King's dependence on Parliament for taxation, deliberately avoiding – at least in the first instance – the provision of a new revenue settlement for Charles. Instead, by persuading the Commons to vote the King the right to collect tonnage and poundage on a two-monthly basis only, Pym ensured that Charles kept coming cap in hand to the MPs. This was a circumstance that meant that it was possible to attach unpalatable propositions to the request for money and to coerce the King, a procedural method that had failed spectacularly in the 1620s.

Pym also advanced his programme by shrewd use of committees, to which he referred vital issues and then dominated the business there through his own agents in order to shape the policy of the Commons as a whole. These committees absorbed the executive functions that had been previously undertaken by Privy Councillors, especially during the parliamentary recess from 9 September to 20 October.

As it began to emerge that a political settlement with Charles would not quickly be attained, Pym was obliged to employ new tactics in order to justify the increasingly radical nature of his reform programme, especially the demand that Charles infuse his Council with advisers nominated by Parliament. First, Pym seems to have developed some form of relationship with the London mob, manipulating them to his advantage by encouraging the circulation of petitions and allowing their spokesmen to address the Commons in order to sustain the programme of reform. 'These political harangues from private citizens were, as far as is known, without precedent and showed how much Pym and the leaders of the House relied on the support of the City parliamentary puritans in the first two years of the Long Parliament.'[24] A petition of 24 April 1641, carrying the names of 20,000 Londoners demanding the death of Strafford must have done much to hasten that event, as must the mob who surrounded Whitehall on 9–11 May and made Charles fear for the life of his Catholic queen. Second, Pym proved himself a master of the judiciously timed revelation, designed to instil a sense of national emergency and consequently garner support for his position. Thus, when it became clear that proceedings against Strafford were in danger of collapsing, Pym revealed his knowledge of the scheme known as the first Army Plot – a design, in which Charles was implicated, to bring the English army south, seize the Tower and allow Strafford to escape. It provoked fury in the Commons. Strode complained that 'ill councell given to a kinge, doth make that King understandeth not what treason is'.[25] The resulting sense of outrage persuaded the Lords to pass the Act of Attainder by 37 to 11 and the Commons to do the same by 204 to 59.

Similarly, although Pym had become aware of the existence of a second Army Plot (an almost carbon copy of the first) in early June 1641, he chose not to reveal this to the Commons until 30 October, thus diminishing any positive effect for the King of his return to London after his visit to Scotland to sign the Treaty of London.

Nevertheless, despite his persuasive oratory and tactical flair – such as leaving a division until late in the day so that the House was easier to manipulate or insisting that the doors to the chamber be locked in order to heighten the sense of danger – Pym failed to produce a lasting settlement by January 1642. Indeed, because his demands had become more extreme he had alienated some of his supporters, many of whom turned to the King.

Questions

1. 'The reign of King Pym'. To what extent is this a fair assessment of the role of John Pym during the period 1640–1642?
2. Compare and contrast the political strategies of John Pym and Charles I during the period 1640–1642.

SOURCES

1. OUTBREAK OF THE ENGLISH CIVIL WAR

Source A: *His Majesty's Answer to a Printed Book*, 26 May 1642.

[Those responsible for all our troubles are] a faction of Malignant, Schismatical and Ambitious persons, whose design is, and always has been, to alter the frame of the Government both of Church and State, and to subject both King and People to their own lawless arbitrary power and Government.

Source B: from C. H. Firth (ed.), *Memoirs of Edmund Ludlow*, Vol. 1 (Oxford University Press, 1984), pp. 37–8.

[Ludlow's father was a member of the Long Parliament and Edmund replaced him as MP for Wiltshire in 1646. He became a republican and was a signatory of the King's death warrant. His memoirs were written in exile after 1662 and published posthumously in 1698–1699, though, as A. B. Worden has demonstrated, they were significantly edited – indeed altered – by an anonymous editor in order to serve the political propaganda purposes of the day.]

... a parliament now being called ... and it being clear to them that the King would do nothing effectual to redress the present, or to secure the people from future mischiefs, choosing rather to contend with them by arms, than for their satisfaction to entrust the militia in faithful hands ... I thought it my duty ... to enter into the service of my country in the army commanded by the earl of Essex under the authority of Parliament.

Source C: *His Majesty's Declaration for all his Loving Subjects*, published December 1641.

We shall in a few words pass over ... the many good laws passed by our Grace and favour this Parliament for the security of our people: of which we shall only say this much, that as we have not refused to pass any Bill presented to us by our Parliament for redress of those grievances mentioned in the [Grand] Remonstrance, so we have not had a greater Motive for the passing those laws than our own resolution (grounded upon our observation, and understanding the state of our Kingdom) to have freed our subjects for the future, from those pressures which were grievous to them if those laws had not been propounded which therefore we shall as inviolably maintain, as we look to have our Rights preserved.

Source D: the petition accompanying the Grand Remonstrance, presented to the King on 1 December 1641.

Most Gracious Sovereign, your Majesty's most humble and faithful subjects, the Commons in this present Parliament assembled, do with much thankfulness and joy acknowledge the great mercy and favour of God, in giving your Majesty a safe and peaceful return out of Scotland into your Kingdom of England . . . The duty which we owe to your Majesty and our country cannot but make us very sensible and apprehensive that the multiplicity, sharpness and malignity of those evils under which we have now many years suffered, are fomented and cherished by a corrupt and ill-affected party, who [have employed various] mischievous devices . . . to get themselves a party and faction among your subjects.

Questions

*1. How similar are the explanations offered by Sources A and D for the problems that afflicted England at this time? [2]

2. With reference to Source C, how convincing do you find Ludlow's assertion in Source B that 'the King would do nothing effectual to redress the present . . . mischiefs'? [3]

3. With reference to the tone and language of Sources C and D, compare the effectiveness with which Parliament and the King appeal for support. [4]

4. Read Source B. Why should a historian be cautious about accepting Ludlow's account of events? [4]

5. Using these sources and your own knowledge, to what extent do you agree with the notion that the main reason why the English Civil War occurred was because each side believed in a conspiracy theory? [7]

Worked answer

*1. [This question carries only 2 marks and therefore the response should be brief.]

According to Sources A and D the explanations for England's difficulties are very similar. Each articulates a belief that the 'troubles' and 'evils' under which the country suffered were the result of the machinations of certain 'persons'. Source A's reference to a malignant 'faction' is echoed by D's concern regarding 'a corrupt and ill-affected party', though the sources are not referring to the same faction.

SOURCES

2. THE METHODOLOGY OF PYM

Source E: Clarendon's *History of the Rebellion*.

Mr Hyde met Mr Pym in Westminster Hall some days before the parliament, and conferring together upon the state of affairs, the other told him [Hyde] 'that they must now be of another temper than they were the last parliament . . . that they had now an opportunity to make their country happy, by removing all grievances, and pulling up the causes of them by the roots, if all men would do their duties' . . . by which it was discerned that the warmest and boldest counsels would find a much better reception than those of a more temperate nature.

Source F: from Pym's speech to the preliminary charges against Strafford, 25 November 1640.

It is far from the Commons to desire any abridgement of those great prerogatives which belong to the King; they know that their own liberty and peace are preserved and secured by his prerogative . . . A king and his people make one body: the inferior parts confer nourishment and strength, the superior sense and motion. If there be an interruption of this necessary intercourse of blood and spirits, the whole body must needs be subject to decay and distemper.

Source G: from a report of John Pym's speech in Parliament on 5 November 1641 in the journal of Sir Simonds D'Ewes.

Mr Pym stood up and moved that no man should be more ready than himself to engage his estate, person, life and all for the suppression of this rebellion in Ireland . . . But he feared that as long as the king gave ear to those evil counsellors about him all that we did would prove in vain, and therefore he desired that we might add some declaration . . . that howsoever we had engaged ourselves for the assistance of Ireland, yet unless the king would remove his evil counsellors and take such counsellor as might be approved by parliament, we should account ourselves free from this engagement.

Source H: Article One of the impeachment issued against Pym and five others in January 1642.

That they have traitorously endeavoured to subvert the fundamental laws and government of the kingdom of England, to deprive the King of his regal power.

Questions

1. Read Source E. What had been the 'temper' of the 'last parliament'? [2]
2. What do Sources E, F and G tell you about the political methods of John Pym? [3]
*3. Compare the tone of Sources F and G. With reference to the provenance of these sources and your own knowledge account for the differences between the two sources. [5]
4. Is there any evidence in these sources to support the impeachment article, Source H? [3]
5. Using these sources and your own knowledge, to what extent would you agree with the remark that 'John Pym was the instigator of the English Civil War'? [7]

*3. Worked answer

The tone of Source F is conservative, conciliatory and deferential. Pym alleges that the Commons did not 'desire any abridgement of those great prerogatives which belong to the King'. He also asserts that the 'superior' parts of the constitution imbue the system with the qualities of 'sense and motion'. In contrast, the tone of Source G is strident and intimidatory. On this occasion Pym is blackmailing the King into relinquishing his 'evil counsellors' and demanding instead that he employ 'such counsellor[s] as might be approved by parliament', otherwise the Commons will 'account ourselves free' from assisting the King in putting down the Irish rebellion. Clearly, this threat represented an extraordinary invasion of the monarchical prerogative and is therefore a direct contradiction of Pym's earlier statement.

There are two main ways in which the differences between Sources F and G may be explained. First, Source G was produced almost twelve months after Source F. In the meantime a number of events had occurred that seemed to suggest that the King could not be trusted, in particular the fact that Charles had been implicated in the Army Plots, the Incident and the Antrim Plot. Since it now seemed that Charles could not be relied upon to maintain the concessions that he had already made, such as agreeing to call a Parliament at least once every three years (the Triennial Act of 15 February 1641), Pym was obliged to become more radical in order to secure a lasting settlement. Thus he insisted that the Privy Council be infused with men nominated by Parliament.

Second, the speech of Pym in Source G is from the Journal of Sir Simonds D'Ewes. As a piece of reported speech it is possible that it may not be fully reliable, though its content seems to be affirmed by Source H.

3

THE WAR MACHINES, 1642–1646

BACKGROUND NARRATIVE

On 10 January 1642, shortly after his descent upon the House of Commons in an attempt to arrest the Five Members, Charles I departed London. Thereafter, he was to spend the rest of his life trying to regain the capital, sometimes by diplomatic means but more often by force.

On 23 February the King bade farewell to his wife, Henrietta Maria. Her exile on the Continent was designed not only for her personal safety but as a means to aid the raising of resources for the Royalist cause. However, in this latter role Henrietta was to prove largely ineffectual, her requests for aid thwarted by the pervasive sense of exhaustion that was a consequence of the Thirty Years War. Meanwhile, Charles had travelled to the north of England only to be denied entry to Hull – the site of a considerable arsenal – by Sir John Hotham on 23 April. Even upon raising his standard at Nottingham on 22 August there was a palpable lack of enthusiasm for the King's cause. Nevertheless, having travelled to the Welsh Marches and West Midlands, Charles began to enjoy a level of support that enabled him to field a considerable army. Though most historians consider that the outcome of the Battle of Edgehill (23 October) was a draw, it was in at least one way a draw in Charles's favour: the road to London lay open. However, apparently bereft of a sense of urgency, the Royalists descended upon the capital not only too late in the season but after a period of time that had allowed their opponents to marshal their resources. Thus, on 13 November the royal advance on London was halted at Turnham Green. Charles subsequently retreated and established his headquarters at Oxford.

A series of Royalist victories in 1643 – Adwalton Moor (30 June), Lansdown (5 July), Roundway Down (13 July) and the fall of Bristol (26 July) – seemed indicative of a looming Parliamentarian collapse and proof to the King that he had been correct in his decision not to agree terms in the peace talks that had been held at Oxford from February to April. However, on 8 September the commander-in-chief of the Parliamentarian forces, Lord General Essex, relieved Gloucester from a Royalist siege. Twelve days later he halted the King's advance towards London at the first Battle of Newbury.

With the onset of stalemate and the prospect of a war of attrition, both sides sought allies. On 15 September 1643 Ormonde, the King's representative in Ireland, concluded a 'cessation' (renegotiated in 1645) with the Irish Confederates – those who were rebelling against English government of Ireland. Thus, between October 1643 and June 1644 a total of around 22,000 troops, both English and native Irish, descended upon England, Wales and Scotland. However, arriving in a piecemeal fashion, they were especially vulnerable to the Parliamentarian elements. Sir Thomas Fairfax routed such a force at Nantwich on 25 January 1644. Henceforth, having formed an alliance with the Covenanting Scots – the Solemn League and Covenant – on 25 September 1643, the tide seemed to turn in favour of Parliament. In particular, aided by a Scottish force of 22,000, Parliament gained control of the north of England after defeating Royalist forces at Marston Moor on 2 July 1644. However, it was a hollow victory since a large number of the Covenanting Scots, threatened by the activities of Scottish Royalists operating under the leadership of Montrose, returned home.

The defeat of Essex at Lostwithiel on 2 September 1644, and his role in the indecisive second Battle of Newbury on 27 October, encouraged Parliament to reform its armies. The outcome was the formation of the New Model Army, a force that defeated the King decisively at Naseby on 14 June 1645. Thereafter, with Montrose finally overcome at Philiphaugh on 13 September, it was only a matter of time before Charles was forced to give up the struggle. On 5 May 1646 the King surrendered his person to the Scots at Newark.

ANALYSIS (1): 'PARLIAMENT DID NOT WIN THE FIRST CIVIL WAR 1642–1646, THE KING LOST IT'. TO WHAT EXTENT DO YOU AGREE WITH THIS ASSERTION?

The first part of this essay will compare initial Royalist advantages with Parliamentarian disadvantages. However, in order fully to answer this question, the second part of the essay will compare Royalist disadvantages with Parliamentarian advantages. From this it will be seen that Parliament was almost certain to win a war of long duration.

In the first instance the Royalist cause benefited from a unified high command and a monarch who was prepared to march at the head of his army. Moreover, as commander-in-chief, Charles was not lacking in either personal bravery or tactical agility, assets he demonstrated at, for example, the Battles of Cropredy Bridge (29 June 1644) and Lostwithiel (2 September 1644). The King's cause was also aided by the fact that it aimed at achieving a particular strategic objective: the taking of London. Indeed, in 1643 Charles seems to have developed a military strategy that was designed to fulfil this end. Three separate field armies were to descend upon the capital – Sir Ralph Hopton from the south-west, the Earl of Newcastle from Yorkshire and Charles himself from the Midlands. Above all, the fact that Charles was a divinely ordained authority possessing an established position in the seventeenth-century constitution meant that he was more easily able to establish the executive bodies necessary to the organisation and direction of the royal war effort.

The most important of these, responsible for both administering the war effort and advising the King in strategic decision making, was the Council of War at the Royalist military headquarters in Oxford. 'In 1644, particularly,' observes Ian Roy, 'the Council proved flexible in its strategic thinking, and efficient in carrying it into practice.'[1] Meanwhile, in order to raise the provinces on his behalf, Charles relied upon the medieval device of the Commission of Array – a royal instrument sent to named men in every county empowering them to take control of the local militia and to collect contributions of money and armed men and send them to the King. It was to the King's advantage that soldiers raised by this device (unlike the Lieutenancy) could legally be moved beyond their county borders.

Parliament, on the other hand, was faced with the difficulty of having to create an executive machinery from scratch. Its solution was to design a series of central committees consisting mainly of members of both Houses, the most important of which was the Committee of Safety, established in July 1642 (later the Committee of Both

Kingdoms after Parliament allied with the Scots in 1643) and charged with advising the Lord General. Yet it was never made clear whether it was the MPs or the commander of the field armies, Lord General Essex, who held the ultimate responsibility in terms of strategic decision making. This grey area certainly seems to have contributed to the disaster at Lostwithiel.

Both sides had expected the war to be short and decisive. However, even when it became apparent after the drawn Battle of Edgehill and the stand-off at Turnham Green on 13 November 1642 that this would not be the case, Parliament proved reluctant to rethink fundamental aspects of its organisation. In particular, since it had resolved that the local militia – under the control of the Lords Lieutenants and Deputy Lieutenants who were directly answerable to Parliament – would concentrate on local defence and that the field army of 20,000 foot and 5,000 horse should operate independently under the command of Essex, it was henceforth logistically difficult for the two sets of forces to combine. Even when Parliament created new regional armies by grouping counties together – the Eastern Association, for example, was an amalgamation of the militia in Norfolk, Suffolk, Essex, Cambridgeshire and Hertfordshire established on 20 December 1642 – it limited their effectiveness by reserving all the appointments to these association armies to Essex. The result was a tangled web of resentments and misunderstandings that the Committee of Both Kingdoms spent much time arbitrating. Moreover, these regional armies did little to overcome the entrenched localism of the militia. Oliver Cromwell's regiment in the Eastern Association was depleted because of the 'erroneous opinion . . . of our unexperienced country soldiers that they ought not to be drawn or ledd . . . beyond the bounds of the five counties'.[2] This problem was offset to some degree because the Royalist cause, which also created association armies, suffered similarly.

Unlike the supporters of the King, Parliamentarians were not united in pursuit of a particular objective. Indeed, especially after the re-entry of the Scots into English affairs in 1643, there appeared a polarisation of opinion among MPs and commanders as to how the war should be concluded. On the one hand, the Political Presbyterians desired to create circumstances in which the King would be compelled to assent to some sort of compromise agreement. On the other hand, the Political Independents were determined to defeat the King militarily and then impose harsh terms along the lines of the Nineteen Propositions of 1642.[3] This division of Parliament and its forces into 'peace' and 'war' factions was at least in part the cause of both the failure to consolidate success after defeating the northern Royalist forces at the Battle of Marston Moor on 2 July 1644 and the draw from a winning position at the second Battle of Newbury on 27 October 1644. Indeed, Cromwell later alleged that the Earl of Manchester, the commander of the Eastern Association, 'hath always been indisposed and backward to engagements and the ending of the War by the sword'.[4] Even Essex himself was accused of the same, leading some MPs to demand his replacement by Sir William Waller. One wit described the situation in verse:

> Farewell, my Lord of Essex, with hey,
> Farewell, my Lord of Essex, with ho,
> He sleeps till eleven,
> And leaves the cause till six or seven,
> But 'tis no matter – their hope's in
> heaven!
> With a hey, trolly, lolly, ho![5]

Yet it would be erroneous to conclude from this that the King lost the war because he failed to consolidate what appeared to be a winning position. Indeed, the Royalist cause suffered from a number of deficiencies.

First, it was perhaps ill-advised for the King to proceed by issuing Commissions of Array since their authority was legally dubious. 'Many did believe', wrote Clarendon, 'that if the King had resorted to the old known way of lords lieutenant and deputy lieutenants, his service would have been better carried on; the commission of array was a thing not before heard of . . . and so was received with jealousy, and easily discredited by the glosses and suggestions of the Houses.'[6] John Morrill has concluded that it amounted to 'a dreadful blunder'.[7]

Second, the authority of the Council of War was confined to those counties near Oxford. Other Royalist territories were therefore commanded largely independently of directives issued by the Council of War: the north of England by the Earl of Newcastle and Lancashire by the Earl of Derby. Charles also appointed four Royalist magnates to serve as regional generals in Wales and the Marches, hoping that their social status rather than any prowess at war would be sufficient to command respect and allegiance. 'The potential disadvantage of such leaders in the field', notes Ronald Hutton, 'had appeared outweighed by their potential advantage in reconciling local people to a war effort.'[8] Yet it was a judgement that proved defective. Of these six grandees, only Newcastle enjoyed success, defeating Fairfax at Adwalton Moor on 30 June 1643.

Third, though both sides experienced difficulties in mobilising resources to furnish their war efforts, the Royalists were at a severe disadvantage in that they controlled the less wealthy territories of England. Moreover, since many of these areas acted as a crucible for the fighting, the consequent deprivation resulted in an inability to pay taxes, convincing John Morrill that 'financial thrombosis [ultimately] killed the Royalist cause'.[9] Nor was the King helped by the fact that Royalist fiscal expedients remained essentially conservative in form. Thus, a 'contribution' was levied by employing the traditional rating lists and was collected by existing local officials only after it had been assented to by a grand jury. In 1644 Charles aped his opponents by instituting an excise tax, but only after it had received the assent of the Royalist Parliament convened at Oxford. Proceeding according to known laws and ancient institutions was inappropriate during a time of war. Nevertheless, by 1645 the Royalists were raising substantial amounts of money – though very little of this arrived at Oxford. As a consequence troops who were paid only infrequently sought free quarter. This in turn induced in the last year of the war the Clubmen movement, rural insurrectionaries determined to protect themselves from plundering soldiers. Since most of the Club risings occurred in Royalist territory they did a great deal to dislocate the war effort of Charles. Thus, 'in the last analysis', notes Ronald Hutton, 'it was the local community, not Parliament, which defeated Charles I, though from hatred of the war itself rather than of the Royalist cause'.[10]

Charles himself was as ineffective as a national leader and general strategist as he was effective on the field of battle. His decision to order his representative in Ireland, Ormonde, to conclude a one-year truce in September 1643 with the Irish Confederates – thus permitting the King to recall his English troops to the mainland – proved disastrous. Not only did it reinforce the perception that the King was prepared to deal with the hated Catholics, but the 22,000 troops whom he received arrived in piecemeal fashion, 2,500 of them being easily beaten by Fairfax at the Battle of Nantwich on 25 January 1644. Despite this, Charles persevered in his efforts to recruit troops from Ireland. When news of an ultimately abortive second cessation treaty of 25 August 1645 leaked out its effect was to bolster Parliament's cause, because many were horrified at the King's willingness to grant concessions to the Catholics in return for arms. Meanwhile, since Montrose had enjoyed an extraordinary run of success against the Covenanters in Scotland from 1644 to 1645, he suggested that the King march to Scotland to ensure a complete Royalist victory north of the border. Instead, Charles chose to engage the New Model

Army, only heading north shortly before Montrose was defeated at Philiphaugh on 13 September 1645.

These setbacks were in part because the King appears to have been impervious to advice offered by the Council of War, though this body was increasingly less effective because of the King's decision to appoint Digby as one of his Secretaries of State in September 1643. The latter was a hardliner and an inveterate rival of another leading member of the Council, Prince Rupert. The Council was further weakened in March 1645 when the King ordered that a Council for the Prince of Wales be set up at Bristol, thus removing from Oxford such experienced councillors as Capel, Culpepper and Hyde.

Yet Parliament's ultimate victory is also explained not just by the deficiencies of the Royalist cause, but by the fact that the Parliamentarians benefited from circumstances and a political vision not enjoyed by their opponents. For instance, whereas the King's war machine was fashioned from traditional institutions and was haltingly cautious in its operation, that of Parliament was at once more flexible, more ruthless and thus more effective. 'They were not tied to a law', commented Lord Wharton in 1643, 'for these were times of necessity and imminent danger.'[11] Henry Parker went even further and asserted that in an emergency the Houses could exercise sovereign powers. Thus, in order to defeat their opponents Parliament breached almost every clause of the Petition of Right.[12] In particular, in 1643 John Pym persuaded his supporters to institute a remarkable series of financial ordinances – weekly assessments (February), sequestrations (March), compulsory loans (May) and the excise (July). Apart from the last, these taxes were collected by county committees staffed by those well affected to Parliament. These devices seem to have been extraordinarily effective, especially the assessment – a land tax roughly equivalent to a parliamentary subsidy every fortnight! Kent, for example, was paying more each month in assessments than it had for an entire year of Ship Money. Despite the fact that these 'illegal' taxes aroused bitter resentment, they increased the incidence with which Parliament paid its troops, a development that in turn perhaps persuaded communities to support Parliament simply because it appeared to be the winning side.

After 1643 Parliament seemed to have the advantage not only in financial terms but also in military respects. The Solemn League and Covenant of September 1643 provided Parliament with military assistance from the Scots. On 1 January 1644 22,000 Covenanters crossed into England and played an important role in the defeat of the Royalist forces at Marston Moor, though thereafter they became something of a paper tiger because of the threat that was posed in Scotland by the Royalist Montrose. Meanwhile, Parliament had passed the Self-denying Ordinance, which stipulated that no member of either House could also enjoy military command (an exception was made for Oliver Cromwell). The removal of Essex and Manchester was accompanied by a reshaping of Parliament's high command and the formation of the New Model Army. Historians have been unable to agree how 'new' this force was, but under the leadership of Sir Thomas Fairfax, with Cromwell as second-in-command, it beat the King decisively at Naseby on 14 June 1645 and then Goring at Langport on 10 July 1645.

Finally, since the processes of taking sides had provided Parliament with the allegiance of much of the richer parts of England, the Ship Money fleet (consisting of 18 men-of-war and 24 armed merchantmen) and, perhaps most importantly, London, it is difficult to avoid the conclusion that in a long war Parliament was almost certain to win. The Ship Money fleet certainly made difficult the passage of munitions from Europe to the Royalist cause but it also meant that Parliamentarian outposts, even those deep in Royalist territory, like Hull and Plymouth, could be victualled by sea. London was significant in a number of ways. First, since there were few presses outside the capital it was important as a centre for propaganda. Second, as the economic and commercial hub of the nation, it was hugely wealthy. For instance, 70 per cent of all customs duties were contributed by London and between one-quarter and one-third of the assessment received by the treasurers derived from the capital. Significantly, the City continued to advance loans against future revenues – almost three-quarters of all Parliamentarian revenues were anticipated in this way. Third, the Trained Bands of London – especially significant at Turnham Green and in lifting the siege of Gloucester in 1643 – were the exception to the rule in that they were well drilled and well officered under the leadership of Philip Skippon. Above all, with a population of about 400,000 – roughly one-tenth of the total population of England – London was a war-winning resource base. At least 6,000 of the initial recruits to Essex's army were from the ranks of the unemployed and religiously committed who swilled around the streets of the capital.

The King's failure to defeat his opponents in 1642–1643 provided Parliament not only with the opportunity to fashion an effective administrative, political and military machine but with the time to mobilise its considerable resources. Since the war was not 'over by Christmas' the advantage thus swung very definitely in favour of Parliament. Nevertheless, even after the Battle of Marston Moor it is possible that the King might yet have won, especially if he had received effective support from either Ireland or Europe. To ensure victory, Parliament therefore had to create a war-winning weapon: the New Model Army.

Questions

1. Why did the First Civil War last so long?
2. 'Once the conflict had become protracted, the King was almost certain to lose.' To what extent do you agree with this remark about the First Civil War?

ANALYSIS (2): HOW NEW WAS THE NEW MODEL ARMY?

The fortunes of the Parliamentarian war effort before and after the creation of the New Model Army in the first months of 1645 are dramatically different. The experience of defeat and disappointment that had been a reasonably constant feature of the first part of the war was replaced by optimism bred by success. The victories of the New Model Army at Naseby (14 June 1645), Langport (10 July 1645) and, latterly, Preston (17–19 August 1648), Dunbar (3 September 1650) and Worcester (3 September 1651) overwhelmed the bitter memories of the humiliation Parliament's field armies had suffered at, for instance, Roundway Down (13 July 1643) and Lostwithiel (2 September 1644). To Cromwell and others, the success of the New Model Army was providential – 'none other than the work of God'.[13]

Until recently, most historians have argued that this success was directly attributable to the fact that, from its inception, the New Model Army was a unique fighting force. 'There had never been anything like the New Model Army before,' asserts C. Hill.[14] This was an 'army of saints', staffed by officers chosen for their commitment to a godly reformation rather than their social origins. Give me a 'plain russet-coated captain that knows what he fights for, and loves what he knows, than that which you call a gentleman and is nothing else,' pleaded Cromwell.[15] Born out of the political tensions of 1644–1645, it has also been seen as the tool of the Independents, designed not only to defeat the King convincingly but to ensure that a form of religious toleration was instituted. Moreover, believing that the rank and file had been infiltrated by the Levellers in the spring of 1647, historians have argued that this was an army that possessed, from a relatively early stage, its own political agenda and rose in revolt in order to see it implemented.

However, Mark Kishlansky has contended that at its creation the New Model Army 'marked no break with Parliament's past, no ascendancy of a "win-the-war" policy, and no feat of administrative genius'.[16] This was, he argues, a predominantly secular force, not an 'army of saints'. Moreover, Kishlansky asserts that the radicalisation of the New Model Army came about only late in 1647, and then very quickly. He believes that the army revolted, not because it had been infiltrated by the Levellers who induced the soldiers to act out a deeply held political and religious ideology, but because the material grievances of the soldiers made the army ripe for revolt − a revolt which eventually occurred because of Parliament's refusal to provide the soldiers' arrears of pay and indemnity. Therefore, according to the revisionist position, the New Model Army, at least in the first two years or so of its existence, barely deserves its adjectival prefix.

Of central importance to the older interpretation is the notion that the Self-denying Ordinance of 3 April 1645 − which disqualified members of both the Commons and Lords from all civil and military offices − was contrived and implemented by the Independents, that element which wanted to defeat the King decisively and enjoy liberty to tender consciences. A number of contemporaries recorded the belief that the Self-denying Ordinance was the result of a plot by the Independents in order to gain for themselves an army under Cromwell, a notion that seems to be supported by the fact that Cromwell was exempted from its terms. However, it has been pointed out that it was very unlikely that Cromwell could have expected Parliament to exempt him personally from its terms.[17] Rather, it seems that he was prepared to sacrifice his military career in order to witness the destruction of the Earl of Manchester. Moreover, even when he was appointed as Lieutenant-General of the Horse he never received a permanent exemption from the provisions of the Self-denying Ordinance.[18]

Kishlansky has argued that the Self-denying Ordinance could not have been the ambition of a particular 'party' in Parliament because the necessity of defeating the King meant that politics in 1645 were still more consensual than adversarial. The Self-denying Ordinance 'was (thus) intended to purify the parliamentary movement using methods of consensus to reunite bickering parliamentarians'.[19] This is supported by the fact that Presbyterians and Independents seem to have been balanced against each other in the appointments to high command in the New Model Army and the fact that the collapse of peace negotiations at Uxbridge in February 1645 meant that effective prosecution of the war was the only viable political strategy.[20]

Nevertheless, it cannot be denied that the passage of the Self-denying Ordinance imbued the New Model Army with an innovative character; since it meant that Parliament dismissed all of its aristocratic military leadership this could hardly be otherwise. Yet the change does appear to have been one of style rather than substance. For the large part, the New Model Army was formed from a merger of the forces of the existing field armies. Of the 14,400 infantry required, 3,048 of these men came from Essex's infantry, 3,578 from Manchester's and 600 from Waller's army. The remainder – including the 1,000 dragoons that were required – was made up largely by impressment.[21] The cavalry regiments of 6,600 troopers came almost entirely from the Eastern Association army, many of whom resented having to serve outside the association area and thus inhibited the New Model Army from acting as a national force. It follows from this that the majority of the officers were experienced soldiers. 'I call it the new Army not because any new officers are to be chosen, for there are only such . . . who are already in the service,' remarked one newswriter.[22] In fact, 8 of the 24 colonels had served in Essex's army and 11 under Manchester.[23] Nor, as its detractors argued, were these men low-born 'tradesmen, brewers, tailors, goldsmiths, shoemakers and the like'.[24] Rather, it has been calculated that out of 37 colonels and general officers, 21 were commoners of good family, 9 were members of noble families and only 7 were not gentlemen by birth.[25] In other words, appointment to the highest positions continued to be made essentially according to nobility rather than ability, though promotion – and sometimes recruitment to the lower orders – seems to have occurred according to the latter principle.

Nor was the organisation of the New Model Army in any way unique. As before, military decisions originated at Westminster in the Committee of Both Kingdoms, on which the deposed generals Essex and Manchester continued to sit, rather than in any Councils of War held in the field. Moreover, as had been the case with Essex, it remained unclear how the authority of Fairfax – the Lord General of the New Model Army – related to that of commanders of other regional armies that continued to exist, particularly Massey's Western Army and Poyntz's Northern Army.

The new army was also financed on the basis of the existing monthly assessment which, in 1645, amounted to £53,000 but later rose to £60,000 and then £120,000 in 1649 – the yearly equivalent of roughly twenty-four pre-war parliamentary subsidies. What is important in this respect is the fact that the New Model Army was more generously financed than Parliament's other armies, allowing it to become more professional than any of its predecessors. Indeed, between its founding (in April 1645) and June 1647 the foot were paid 76 per cent and the cavalry 58 per cent of the time; by seventeenth-century standards this was a remarkable record.[26] The fact that the soldiers were paid on a regular basis made them more amenable to a strict code of discipline. 'A general reformation is passed through the army,' remarked Henry Walker, 'no oaths nor cursing, no drunkenness, nor quarrelling but love, unanimity is amongst them. I have been in the army an eye witness of their admirable carriages.'[27]

The success of the New Model in the period 1645–1646 therefore seems to be accounted for more by the errors of its opponents combined with an acknowledgement of the fact that it was well paid rather than because of any war-winning 'newness' it possessed. Yet the notion that there was little that was distinctive about the New Model Army in 1645 apart from its uniform – the famous redcoat edged with blue – has not gone unchallenged. In particular, Ian Gentles has demonstrated that the New Model Army was composed of a high proportion of volunteers among the cavalry units, and that these men – in contrast to the conscripts in the infantry – joined in order to fight for a cause. He argues that their radical religious zeal disproves Kishlansky's assertion that 'secular domination' was the salient feature of the New Model Army. Instead, it possessed a 'peculiar religious stamp' from its inception which in turn meant that the greater part of the army's membership was driven by a religious ideology, a Calvinistic Puritanism that enabled the soldiers to challenge their King effectively.[28] Gentles insists that it was this ideology that 'liberated them psychologically, transformed them into men of iron, endowed them with a holy ruthlessness, and furnished them with the invincible belief that in turning their own society upside down and exporting their revolution to Ireland and Scotland they were performing the will of God'.[29] As one contemporary remarked, 'Men conquer better as they are saints, than soldiers.'[30]

Widely differing interpretations among historians make it a difficult task to quantify the 'newness' of the New Model Army. Perhaps it is safe to conclude that the findings of Gentles make it clear that the army was a good deal 'newer' than the arguments of Kishlansky would have us believe.

Questions

1. 'What proved to be new about the New Model Army was less its fighting qualities than its political and religious convictions.'

Discuss this opinion of the New Model Army with reference to the years 1645–1648.

2. To what extent do you agree with Kishlansky's assertion that at its creation the New Model Army 'marked no break with Parliament's past, no ascendency of a "win-the-war" policy, and no feat of administrative genius'?

SOURCES

1. THE IMPACT OF THE WAR

Source A: a remonstrance sent to Parliament from the Northern Association shortly after the end of the First Civil War.

We daily groan under the unsupportable weight of oppressive taxes, free-quarter (besides murder, rapine, robberies, not mentioning the deep exhaustings during the late time of war . . .) we humbly desire a speedy alleavement and retardation thereof, that yet . . . we may have bread to sustain the lives of our poor wives and children, many thousands being ready to perish through want . . . else we shall be enforced through necessity (heaven knows our unwillingness) to acquit ourselves (by the readiest way) of our [not] any longer tolerable calamities, and purchase freedom, though with the sacrifice of our dearest blood.

Source B: a description of the sacking of Birmingham by a Royalist force in the spring of 1643.

Having thus possessed themselves of the town, they ran into every house, cursing and damning themselves most hideously . . . [and] they beastly assaulted many women's chastity.

Source C: Sir Anthony Ashley Cooper describes an assault upon a fortified house by his Parliamentarian troops, October 1644.

. . . and then they cried for quarter, but having beat diverse men before it, and considering how many garrisons of the same nature we had to deal with, I gave command that there should be none given.

Source D: extract from the *Commonplace Book of William Davenport of Bramhall*, 1643–1645.

In May 1644 . . . came Prince Rupert and his army, by whom I lost better than 100 pounds in Linens and other goods at Milesend, besides the rifling and pulling in pieces of my house. By them and my Lord Goring's army, I lost eight horses and besides victuals and other provisions they ate me three score bushels of oats. No sooner was the prince gone but Stanley's cornet, one Lely, and 20 of his troop hastened their return to plunder me of my horses which the prince had left me, which he did.

Source E: the assessment charged on London and the English counties (along with the Ship Money they had been expected to pay in the 1630s).

Place	Yearly assessment charge, £	Yearly Ship Money charge, £
Bedfordshire	13,000	3,000
Berkshire	28,600	4,000
Buckinghamshire	21,840	4,500
Cambridgeshire	19,500	3,500
Cheshire	9,110	3,500
Cornwall	32,500	6,500
Cumberland	1,950	1,000*
Derbyshire	9,100	3,500
Devon	96,226	9,000
Dorset	22,984	5,000
Durham	3,250	2,000
Essex	58,500	8,000
Gloucestershire	42,250	5,500
Hampshire	39,000	6,000
Herefordshire	22,750	4,000
Hertfordshire	23,400	4,000
Huntingdonshire	11,440	2,000
Kent	65,000	8,000
Lancashire	26,000	3,500
Leicestershire	9,750	4,500
Lincolnshire	42,250	8,000
London	520,000	1,600
Middlesex	39,000	5,500
Norfolk	65,000	8,000
Northamptonshire	22,100	6,000
Northumberland	2,600	3,000
Nottinghamshire	9,750	3,500
Oxfordshire	33,800	3,500
Rutland	3,250	1,000

continued . . .

Place	Yearly assessment charge, £	Yearly Ship Money charge, £
Shropshire	19,500	4,500
Somerset	54,600	8,000
Staffordshire	11,050	2,000
Suffolk	65,000	8,000
Surrey	20,800	4,000
Sussex	32,500	5,000
Warwickshire	29,250	4,000
Westmorland	1,417	1,000**
Wiltshire	37,700	7,000
Worcestershire	28,600	4,000
Yorkshire	55,250	12,000

Notes: * Shared with Westmorland
** Shared with Cumberland

Questions

1. Read Source C. How does Cooper justify his decision that no quarter should be given? [2]
2. To what extent are the complaints voiced by the authors of Source A supported by Sources B, C, D and E? [5]
*3. With reference to tone and content, comment upon the effectiveness of Source A's appeal to Parliament. [5]
4. How useful do you consider Source E to be for the historian researching the financial burden of the First Civil War? [6]
5. With reference to Sources A to E, and your own knowledge, to what extent would you agree with the assertion that the First Civil War was a disaster for civilians? [7]

Worked answer

*3. In order that Parliament might be more likely to effect an 'alleavement and retardation' of the effects of the war, the petitioners initially adopt a deferential tone, 'humbly' beseeching Parliament's assistance. However, the tone of the remonstrance then becomes melodramatic, seeking a redress of grievances through emotional blackmail. Parliament is warned that 'many thousands' are 'ready to perish through want' and that the only way that '[in]tolerable calamities' of this sort can be thwarted is by 'the sacrifice of our dearest blood' –

killing of the weakest. This is dramatic and effective, suggesting that unless Parliament takes action circumstances will mean that the 'petitioners will be enforced through necessity' to desperate courses.

SOURCES

2. THE ORIGINS OF THE NEW MODEL ARMY

Source F: extract from Lucy Hutchinson, *Memoirs of the Life of Colonel Hutchinson* (1664–1671).

It was too apparent how much the whole parliament cause had been often hazarded, how many opportunities of finishing the war had been overslipped by the Earl of Essex's army; and it was believed that he himself with his commanders rather endeavoured to become arbiters of war and peace than conquerors for the parliament, for it was known that he had given out such expressions.

Source G: deposition of Sir Arthur Haselrig, 6 December 1644.

The Earl of Manchester said . . . 'that if we beat the King ninety and nine times yet he is King still, and so will his posterity be after him, but if the King beat us once we shall be all hanged, and our posterity made slaves'. These were the very words as this examinant remembers.

Source H: 'Cromwell's Narrative' (25 November 1644).

I did . . . freely declare that I thought the Earl of Manchester was most in fault for most of those miscarriages [of the war] and the ill consequences of them. And because I had a great deal of reason to think that his Lordship's miscarriage in these particulars was neither through accidents . . . nor through his improvidence only, but through his backwardness to all action, and . . . that backwardness was not merely from dullness or indisposedness [disinclination] to engagement, but . . . from . . . unwillingness to have this war prosecuted unto a full victory, and a design or desire to have it ended by accommodation, and that on such terms to which it might be disadvantageous to bring the King too low.

Source I: Self-denying Ordinance, 3 April 1645.

Be it ordained by the Lords and Commons assembled in Parliament, that all and every of the members of either House of Parliament shall be . . . discharged at the end of forty days after the passing of this Ordinance of and from all and every office or command military or civil, granted or conferred by both or either of the said Houses of this present Parliament.

Questions

1. Give two examples of 'opportunities' for 'finishing the war' being 'overslipped' by the Earl of Essex's army during the period 1642–1644. [2]
2. Read Sources F, G and H. How similar are the attitudes to the war of Essex and Manchester as portrayed by these accounts? [5]
3. Read Source G. How reliable is this source as evidence of Manchester's attitude towards the war? [6]
*4. Read Sources F, H and I. To what extent were the concerns expressed by Hutchinson (F) and Cromwell (H) alleviated by the Self-denying Ordinance (I)? [4]
5. 'The most important aspect of Parliament's new modelling of their army was the Self-denying Ordinance.' To what extent do you agree with this remark? Refer to these sources and your own knowledge in your answer. [8]

Worked answer

*4. Hutchinson and Cromwell articulate similar concerns. Both are worried that Parliament's war effort has suffered from missed opportunities, Hutchinson alleging that occasions when Parliament might have brought the war to an end 'had been overslipped' while Cromwell records his concern about the 'ill consequences' of 'mis-carriages' of the war. It is also apparent that both writers believe that Parliament's commanders have contrived through 'backwardness' (Source H) 'to become arbiters of war and peace', rather than 'conquerors for the parliament' (Source F). In other words, both believe that there is a general reluctance to defeat the King on the field of battle.

Thus, Cromwell and Hutchinson seem likely to have been delighted by the terms of the Self-denying Ordinance (Source I) since it 'dis-charged' all those who were currently commanding Parliament's armies, including Essex and Manchester. On the other hand, Cromwell may have been less than enthusiastic because he too was to be affected by its terms – though he was ultimately made an exception to its provisions.

4

THE VICTORS FALL OUT AND THE EMERGENCE OF RADICALISM, 1646–1649

BACKGROUND NARRATIVE

Charles had deliberately chosen to surrender his person to the Scots in May 1646 in the expectation that this would exacerbate the tensions that were emerging between the various elements of the coalition that had defeated him. On the one hand, Parliament and the Scots were embroiled in an increasingly antagonistic relationship, in the large part a result of Parliament's failure to institute what the Scots thought had been agreed in the Solemn League and Covenant of 25 September 1643 – that is, the establishment of a full Presbyterian Church in England, a form of ecclesiastical settlement in which, among other things, all ministers were regarded as equal and operated according to a rigid structure of discipline based on the Calvinist institutions of a national synod, regional assemblies and local groupings of parishes called presbyteries. On the other hand, the New Model Army was aggrieved by Parliament's reluctance to pay its arrears and provide an Act of Indemnity – exemption from any penalties either that the King might impose on those who had fought against him or prosecution by private individuals who had lost property to the Parliamentarian armies. There were also serious differences, especially in terms of religion, between the Scots and the New Model Army.

Thus, fearful that the Covenanting Scots might independently come to terms with the King, Parliament was obliged to accommodate the war aims of their erstwhile allies in the terms that they presented to Charles on 13 July 1646. The Newcastle Propositions therefore stipulated that Charles was to take the Covenant and agree to the abolition of bishops. Other important terms stated that Parliament was to nominate thirteen key officers of state and to control the militia for the next twenty years. Charles was also obliged to give his consent to fifty-eight Royalists being excluded from pardon. Yet, by incorporating Scottish demands in their terms for a settlement it was inevitable that Parliament would disaffect the New Model Army. Therefore, since no one could yet contemplate a settlement without the King, the army was provoked into offering its own terms to Charles in July 1647. Though the Heads of the Proposals were in every respect more lenient than the Newcastle Propositions, the King nevertheless chose to decline them, anticipating that royal intransigence would continue to divide his enemies and thus allow him ultimately to rule as before.

Charles's decision was bolstered by the fact that divisions within each of the various groups that made up the victorious coalition were becoming increasingly apparent. In Scotland there was a growing reaction against the Covenanters, a process advanced by the defeat of Covenanting forces in Ireland on 5 June 1646 at Benburb. Meanwhile, Parliament was divided between the Independents and Presbyterians, groups of MPs who, among other things, advocated respectively a wide measure of religious toleration and desired a national Church similar to the Presbyterian system in Scotland. The New Model Army also began to suffer internal problems. In the summer of 1647 there were clashes between, on the one hand, the rank and file led by Agitators and, on the other, the officers, or Grandees. These differences were made more serious because the Agitators were motivated by a political ideology espoused by various radical groups, but especially the Levellers.

ANALYSIS (1): WHY DID A SETTLEMENT PROVE SO ELUSIVE DURING THE PERIOD 1645–1647?

In the months after the Battle of Naseby in 1645 Charles suffered a series of crushing blows: defeat at Langport (10 July); the surrender of Bristol (10 September); the final collapse of Montrose at Philiphaugh (13 September) and the apparent demise of any prospect of securing the services of an Irish or Continental army. Though convincingly defeated in the field of battle, a lasting settlement between the King and his victors was only really obtainable if all parties were prepared to compromise their respective positions. Yet compromise was a rare commodity in the eighteen months after Charles surrendered his person to the Scots at Newark on 5 May 1646.

As is usual, the defeat of the common enemy revealed substantial differences between the various elements of the victorious coalition. Indeed, acrimonious haggling over the possession of the King's person and money meant that the Scots and Parliament were on the brink of war as early as 1646. Above all, there were disputes between these two parties over religion, the Scots lamenting that Parliament eventually erected no more than 'a lame Erastian Presbytery' – an ecclesiastical settlement in which the national synod, instead of being independent, was obliged to operate in close association with Parliament. Then, after the politicisation of the New Model Army in 1647, Parliament had to cope with a military force that, declaring itself 'no mere mercenary army', espoused its own political programme.[1] Moreover, for as long as settlement was delayed, differences grew between factions within each of these elements – in Parliament between the Presbyterians and the Independents, in Scotland between the hardline Covenanters and Engagers (disparate groups of Royalists, neutrals and moderate Covenanters led by Hamilton) and in the army between the Grandees and the rank and file. As a result there was remarkably little agreement among the victors about what sort of shape any peace terms should take; the question of the nature of the religious settlement was perhaps the most divisive issue.

Settlement therefore proved elusive because it was extremely difficult for any single faction to produce terms to which a majority of its wartime allies was prepared to give support. Furthermore, the adversaries of the King could not easily soften any terms that they did present but which were turned down. After all, Parliament's Newcastle Propositions contained clauses that were constitutionally harsh at least in part to satisfy the Independents.[2] Meanwhile, their demand that the King assent to the establishment of a Presbyterian Church was designed to appease not only the Presbyterian MPs but, more especially, the Scots. Similarly, the Heads of the Proposals – in that they offered liberty to tender consciences – were designed to command support from both the Independents and the army.[3] Neither Parliament nor the army could therefore offer concessions. For either to have improved its terms in the hope of winning the assent of the King would only have further fragmented what little unity existed and ultimately deprived each of the support necessary to impose its terms on the other.

If circumstances prevented the victors from making concessions, then the King was prevented from so doing largely by 'conscience and honour'. The latter he believed was already dangerously diminished by the series of concessions he had made to the Long Parliament in 1641 and 1642. He could concede no more, having reached an irreducible core. As for his 'conscience', in a series of letters to Henrietta Maria he made it clear that he 'put little or no difference between setting up the Presbyterian government, or submitting to the Church of Rome' and instructed her that Presbyterianism would destroy secular as well as religious forms of government.[4] He was wedded and glued to the preservation of his friends, his Crown and, above all, his Church. 'No bishop, no king,' he insisted. This royal resolve not to make concessions was bolstered by the negative support that his cause appeared to be receiving from the growing resentment of what was perceived as Parliamentarian tyranny – the continued levy of the excise and assessment, the actions of the county committees and violation of common law principles and traditional local rights by government from the centre. David Underdown has described this period as exhibiting 'a widespread yearning for the good old days, for a return to the old government of J.P.s and locally controlled militias, even at the cost of some crucial elements in the programme for which Parliament had gone to war'.[5]

Since neither side was prepared to offer meaningful concessions the only possible outcome was stalemate, unless perhaps a settlement could proceed without one of the parties. However, it was inconceivable that any of the victorious elements would relinquish their hard-won positions and, moreover, all agreed that no lasting settlement could be made without the person of the King. Indeed, divine-right authority continued to compel respect, even fear. 'If we beat the king ninety and nine times', the Earl of Manchester had said in 1644, 'yet he is king still.'[6] Thus, the Scots dragged their royal prize back to Newcastle in May 1646 and just over a year later the army removed Charles from Holdenby House and the custody of Parliament. It was perhaps less arrogance and more Realpolitik that informed the King when he told the army that 'you cannot be without me; you will fall to ruin if I do not sustain you'.[7]

Though he had lost the war, Charles believed that by prevaricating over the terms with which he was presented he could yet win the peace, especially since the continued absence of any peace dividend seemed likely to culminate in an irresistible popular demand for him to be restored unconditionally. However, Caroline intransigence and duplicity induced a growth of that contingent who argued that if a settlement could not be forged with the King it must be had without him. When Charles rejected Parliament's latest proposals (the Four Bills) on 28 December 1647, having decided instead to form an Engagement on 26 December with a faction of the Scots, the Presbyterians and Independents agreed to break off all negotiations with the King.[8] Upon the passage in the Commons on 3 January 1648 of the Vote of No Addresses forbidding further negotiations with Charles the Second Civil War was henceforth inevitable. The time was growing nearer when Charles I would become Charles the Martyr.

Questions

1. 'A game of divide and rule that almost worked.' Discuss this opinion of the strategy of Charles I following his defeat in the First Civil War.
2. Under what circumstances might a lasting settlement have occurred after the First Civil War?

ANALYSIS (2): 'THE LEVELLER DREAM WAS SHARED BY TOO FEW AND FEARED BY TOO MANY.' IS THIS SUFFICIENT EXPLANATION FOR THE FAILURE OF THE LEVELLERS?

Lacking the statistical information of the sort that the modern-day political commentator has at his fingertips, the historian of the 1640s is obliged instead to assess popularity on the basis of how many names were put to particular petitions and by forming an impression of how many persons appeared on the streets to protest a particular cause. In each respect the Levellers seem to have enjoyed significant support. For example, a petition reiterating the main demands of the Levellers' programme submitted to the Commons on 11 September 1648 is said to have obtained 40,000 signatures. Another, the Remonstrance of Many Thousands of the Free People of England, claimed to have 98,064 signatures. The funerals of Colonel Thomas Rainsborough and

Robert Lockyer, leading Levellers, provoked thousands to march on the streets of London, many of them women.

Meanwhile, other circumstances at this time (1645–1649) seemed to have been working in favour of the Levellers. High-profile leadership existed through the efforts of John Lilburne, William Walwyn, Richard Overton and John Wildman, all of whom had a penchant for writing effective propaganda pieces such as Lilburne's *Englands Birth Right Justified* or Walwyn's *Englands Lamentable Slaverie*. Moreover, the movement benefited from a form of party organisation (at least in London, though a structure also seems to have existed in Buckinghamshire, Hertfordshire and Kent) capable of raising subscriptions and orchestrating large-scale protest. The Levellers also had the advantage of a weekly newspaper, the *Moderate*, which was normally well disposed to their cause and thus provided space for their news and opinions. Finally, a series of poor harvests and general dislocation suffered as a consequence of the Civil Wars served to make the Levellers' opinion and programme particularly apposite. The Levellers, it seemed, were a force with which to be reckoned.

Yet the nature of their programme meant that significant elements of society had no reason to share in their 'dream' and that the established governing element had every reason to be antagonistic towards it. In particular, the latter were outraged by the Leveller attacks on the House of Lords, their demands for drastic reform of the law and calls for the abolition of the Merchant Adventurers and other monopolistic companies. Furthermore, the clergy were alienated by the Levellers' insistence that tithes be abolished. On the other hand, it is true that the 'middling sort' – small tradesmen usually found in towns – welcomed these proposals, and in particular the demand that there be a reformation of the law so that it be 'a just, speedy, plain and unburdensome way for deciding of Controversies'. Of similar appeal was the quest to implement 'some speedy and effectual course to relieve all such prisoners for debt as are altogether unable to pay'.[9] No doubt the Leveller ambition to effect a drastic reduction in taxation and institute universal male suffrage also attracted support to their cause. However, the Levellers offered nothing at all to women and little to those who made up the greater part of society, the lower ranks of the rural populace. A century of inflation and increasingly depressed wages as a result of the growth in population had created a brooding discontent in the countryside. Indeed, in the Midlands in 1607 there had been widespread rioting against enclosure. Yet the Levellers only occasionally advocated the destruction of enclosures, the return of common lands to the people and the abolition of copyhold tenures, the last particularly resented because they were easily manipulated by land-lords. The final Agreement of the People (May 1649) did not mention agrarian problems even though they had grown worse due to a series of catastrophic harvests and the impact of the Second Civil War, not least of which was Parliament's decision to continue to collect the excise tax. 'The Levellers' failure to exploit fully [the grievances of the rural population]', remarks H. Shaw, 'must stand as one of the main reasons why they were defeated so easily.'[10]

That their ultimate defeat was of this nature is, at least upon first examination, somewhat surprising considering the nature of the Levellers' relationship with the New Model Army. Having apparently infiltrated the ranks of the soldiers in the spring of 1647 – though the extent to which this occurred remains controversial – it must have seemed that henceforth the Levellers, or at least their 'dream', would ride to power on the backs of the military. For instance, when the Council of the Army produced the Declaration of the Army on 14 June 1647, famously declaring that 'we are not a mere mercenary army', it insisted that Parliament effect a number of Leveller demands. In particular, it demanded that MPs appoint a date for their own dissolution and make provision for the regular assembly of subsequent Parliaments.[11] Similarly, the peace terms that the army offered to the King in July 1647, the Heads of the Proposals, also contained a number of principles espoused by the Levellers.[12] Moreover, the famous debates between members of the Army Council and Leveller representatives held at Putney in the autumn of 1647 revealed more agreement between the two 'parties' than is normally recognised as being the case.

Yet it seems that Leveller strength in the army was superficial, their apparent success in exerting pressure upon the Grandees being something of an illusion. It is true that the Levellers outlined a course of action, much of which was subsequently followed by the Grandees – such as marching on London, purging Parliament and abolishing the Lords and monarchy – but there were other pressures that compelled the officers to act in these ways, not least of which was the continued duplicity of Charles I and the machinations of the Political Presbyterians. For instance, in July 1647, after a pro-Presbyterian mob forced the flight from Parliament to the army of a large number of Independents, it was the physical presence of the latter that persuaded the Grandees of the necessity of marching on London in August of that year.

Indeed, the relationship between the Grandees and the Levellers was more often antagonistic than it was mutually beneficial. Though

Lilburne had warned the rank and file as early as August 1647 to 'trust your great officers . . . no farther than you can throw an ox', the Leveller leadership seems only late in the day fully to have appreciated that their alliance with the Grandees was built on the temporary weakness of that group rather than implicit Leveller strength.[13] The Grandees simply appeased the Levellers so that they could move against them at some later time. The escape of Charles I from army custody on 11 November 1647 provided the Grandees with a legitimate excuse for using force to extinguish Leveller-inspired discontent in the army. Having called three separate rendezvous rather than one general meeting – thus fatally weakening the radicals – Fairfax and the other officers were able to crush mutinous sentiment that occurred in the rendezvous at Corkbush Field near Ware on 15 November 1647. Lilburne's lament that they had been 'cozened and deceived' – actually a reference to the fact that the Second Agreement of the People had been effectively shelved in January 1649 – is equally appropriate to the circumstances in which the Levellers found themselves in late 1647. Having failed in that year, the Levellers were unlikely ever to succeed.

That the Grandees acted in this way is best understood by a realisation that the core beliefs of the Leveller programme had evolved into the twin demands of religious toleration and sovereignty of the people. Since the attainment of either of these posed a threat to existing property rights they were therefore guaranteed to induce a reactionary fear among members of the established political nation, of whom the Grandees were representatives. Thus, when the Levellers submitted for discussion at Putney their blueprint for a new constitution, the Agreement of the People, one of the Grandees, Henry Ireton, lost no time in attacking its implied advocacy of manhood suffrage (see Source J). He insisted that the franchise be restricted to property owners and warned that manhood suffrage would result in the abolition of property. More generally, the logical consequence of permitting sovereignty to the people was the abolition of the Lords and monarchy, or at least their emasculation by depriving them of their ability to veto legislation (the 'negative voice'). In the stubbornly hierarchical and deferential society that prevailed in seventeenth-century England such a change was not easily contemplated. It would 'turn the world upside down'. The quest for liberty to tender consciences posed a similar threat, for not only would the collapse of a State Church pose problems of disorder, but the abolition of tithes – many of which had been impropriated, acquired by laymen – would threaten the interests of those with property. 'Observe to what this pretended liberty of conscience brings men,' lamented Thomas Edwards in *Gangraena*, 'namely to plead for treason, rebellion and all kinds of wickedness.'[14]

Furthermore, John Morrill has challenged the assumption that there existed an identity of interest between soldier and civilian Leveller. Instead, he has argued that, because the soldiers' resort to free quarter meant that the army was hated by the local communities, only Parliament as it existed possessed the authority required to meet its material demands. In other words, the institution that the Levellers were most desirous of reforming best served the interests of the soldiers. In circumstances where 'Parliament . . . was offering the Army its bread and butter' and 'the Levellers offered them ideological jam', it is Morrill's contention that the rank and file opted for the former.[15]

There are other reasons that help to explain the Levellers' failure. As a political movement it was ideologically and organisationally flawed. For instance, while they lamented all that had transpired since the imposition of the 'Norman Yoke', they nevertheless extolled the virtues of the Magna Carta. They were limited because their influence rarely extended beyond London and the south-east and they also suffered from problems of coordination. Thus, a substantial body of weavers was to have attended the rendezvous at Ware on 15 November 1647 but failed to materialise, and designs to link the revolt at Burford in the spring of 1649 with others came to nothing. 'It is a doleful commentary on the Levellers' talent for organisation', remarks Howard Shaw, 'that their most notable successes were the demonstrations at the funerals of their dead heroes.'[16]

'It has to be said', concludes Austin Woolrych in his account of the defeat of the Levellers, 'the movement was not altogether lucky in its leadership. One could wish that it had taken its cue more from Walwyn . . . than from Lilburne, whose tactical sense was too often clouded by his violent and personal animosities.'[17] Certainly, even though there was no prospect of the Levellers realising their programme by consent, they were unprepared for armed conflict and revolution. The experience of having been put down by force at Ware, and then again at Burford in May 1649, seems to have broken their political resolve. Finally, the Levellers were never really a 'movement'. Even as late as the end of 1646 they were sometimes simply known as 'Lieut-Colonel Lilburne and his friends'. They seem to have been a number of like-minded individuals brought together by circumstances but who disagreed over important details of their programme. When these circumstances disappeared – when the economy improved after 1649, when the new regime granted toleration to the gathered Churches and met the material grievances of the army – much of the *raison d'être* of the Levellers also disappeared.

Thus, the Levellers failed in part because their 'dream' was shared by too few. Howard Shaw concludes that 'it demanded at once too little and too much',[18] while F. D. Dow believes that it 'was too frightening to the rich, too neglectful of the poor and too innovative'.[19] On the other hand, it may not be true to say that the Levellers failed because they were 'feared by too many'; rather, they were feared by those who mattered.

Questions

1. 'The Leveller failure was more a result of their own weaknesses than the strengths of their opponents.' Discuss.
2. To what extent was the Leveller failure a failure of leadership?

SOURCES

1. THE KING IN DEFEAT, 1646

Source A: a letter from Charles I to his wife, 1 July 1646.

[On 28 June 1646] I got a true copy of the London propositions . . . and now do assure thee that they are such as I cannot grasp without loss of my conscience, crown and honour; to which, as I can no way consent, so in my opinion a flat denial is to be delayed as long as may be, and how to make an handsome denying answer is all the difficulty.

Source B: an account of Charles I's first answer to the Newcastle Propositions, 1 August 1646. (Reprinted from the original.)

The propositions tendered to His Majesty by the Commissioners . . . do import so great alterations in government both in the Church and kingdom, as it is very difficult to return a particular and positive answer, before a full debate, wherein these propositions . . . be rightly weighed and understood . . . [However, His Majesty] finds upon discourse with the said Commissioners that they are so bound up from any capacity either to give reasons for the demands they bring, or to give ear to such desires as His Majesty is to propound, as it is impossible for him to give such a present judgement of, and answer to these propositions . . . to which end His Majesty desires and proposeth to come to London.

Source C: a letter from Charles I to the Prince of Wales, Newcastle, 26 August 1646.

Take it as an infallible maxim from me, that, as the Church can never flourish without the protection of the Crown, so the dependency of the Church upon the Crown is the chiefest support of regal authority. This is that which is so well understood by the English and Scots rebels, that no concessions will content them without the change of Church government.

Source D: the King's third answer to the Newcastle Propositions, 12 May 1647.

In answer to all the Propositions concerning religion, His Majesty proposed that he will confirm the Presbyterian government, the Assembly of Divines at Westminster, and the Directory, for three years ... [but] that His Majesty and his household be not hindered from using the form of God's service which they have formerly, and also that a free consultation and debate be had with the Divines at Westminster ... whereby it may be determined by His Majesty, and the two Houses, how the Church shall be governed after the said three years, or sooner if the differences may be agreed.

Touching the Covenant, His Majesty is not therein yet satisfied, and desires to respite his particular answer thereunto until his coming to London.

Questions

1. Why was Charles determined to 'com[e] to London' (Source D)? [2]
2. (i) Read Source B. What is the tone of this, the King's public response to the Propositions? [3]
   (ii) How does this compare with his private response, Sources A and C? [3]
*3. How would an historian go about checking the veracity of the version of events given in Source B? [3]
4. Considering the content of the other sources, how surprised are you by the concessions that Charles eventually offered in Source D? Explain your answer. [4]
5. Refer to these sources and your own knowledge to assess how successful Charles was in forming 'an handsome denying answer' during the period 1646–1647. [10]

Worked answer

*3. Since Source B is a reprint the historian would need to compare this version with the original. He may discover that there have been editorial alterations, such as a modification of language or that perhaps only part of the original has been reprinted. As to the factual content of the source, the historian would need to compare it with details carried in other primary sources. In particular, he would need to read the Newcastle Propositions in order to assess whether they did in fact 'import so great alterations in government', as Charles alleges.

SOURCES

2. THE NATURE OF THE LEVELLERS

Source E: Richard Overton's Remonstrance of Many Thousand Citizens, submitted to the Commons in 1646.

It is high time we be plain with you: ... we do expect, according to reason, that ye should ... declare and set forth King Charles his wickedness openly before the world ... and so to declare King Charles an enemy ... and to convert the great revenue of the crown to the public treasure ... and this we expected long since at your hand ... Ye must also deal better with us concerning the Lords than you have done. Ye only are chosen by us the People and therefore in you only is the power of binding the whole nation by making, altering or abolishing of laws ... We desire you to free us from these abuses ... or else tell us that it is reasonable we should be slaves ... We cannot but expect to be delivered from the Norman bondage ... and from all unreasonable laws made ever since that unhappy conquest; as we have encouragement we shall inform you further, and guide you, as we observe your doings. The work, ye must note, is ours, and not your own ... and therefore you must expect to hear more frequently from us than ye have done; nor will it be your wisdom to take these admonitions and cautions in evil part.

Source F: The Levellers' rant, a Royalist satire on the Levellers, probably written in the 1640s.

'Tis we will pull down what e'er is above us,
And make them to fear, that never did love us;
We'll level the proud, and make every degree
To our royalty bow the knee;
'Tis no less than treason
'Gainst freedom and reason
For our brethren to be higher than we.

Source G: an extract from *The Memoirs of the Life of Colonel Hutchinson*.

[Hutchinson fought for Parliament and *The Life* was composed by his wife in the later 1660s.]

The Lords, as if it were the chief interest of nobility to be licensed in vice, claimed many prerogatives which set them out of the reach of common justice, which these good-hearted people contended to have equally to belong to the poorest as well as the mighty; and for this and other honest declarations were nicknamed Levellers. Indeed, as all virtues are mediums and have their extremes, there rise up after in that name a people who endeavoured the levelling of all estates and qualities which these sober Levellers were never guilty of desiring, but were men of just and sober principles, of honest and religious ends, and therefore hated by all the designing self-interested men ... Colonel Hutchinson had a great intimacy with many of these [sober men].

Source H: from the petition presented by the Levellers to the Commons, 11 September 1648.

The truth is ... we have long expected things of another nature from you:

Article 18. That you would have bound yourselves and all future parliaments from abolishing propriety [property], levelling men's estates and making all things common.

Source I: from Clarendon's *History*.

There was at this time a new faction grown up in the army, which were, either by their own denomination or with their own consent, called Levellers; who spoke insolently and confidently against the King and Parliament and the great officers of the army; professed as great malice against all the lords as against the King, and declared that all degrees of men should be levelled, and an equality should be established, both in titles and estates, throughout the kingdom.

Questions

1. Considering that the suggestion made in Source H was never contemplated by the Commons, why do you think that the Levellers felt it necessary to include this article in their petition? [2]
*2. To what extent is the opinion expressed in Source I supported by the other sources in this collection? [6]
3. Referring to both language and tone, how effective do you find the arguments put forward in Source E? [5]

4. Considering both its content and provenance, how reliable do you consider Source G for the historian researching the Levellers? [4]

5. 'An inappropriate and damaging nickname.' Use these sources and your own knowledge to assess whether this is an appropriate remark about the Levellers. [8]

Worked answer

*2. Source E supports Source I's assertion that the Levellers spoke 'insolently and confidently against the King'. The former is insistent that the Commons should 'set forth' the 'wickedness' of Charles I and 'declare' him as 'an enemy'. This sentiment is also articulated in Source F (unsurprisingly, since it is a Royalist tract) when the author informs his readers that the Levellers wanted to 'pull down what e'er is above us' on the basis that they 'never did love us'. Source E also speaks 'insolently and confidently' against Parliament, a further criticism of the Levellers made by Source I. Thus, the author of Source E informs MPs that the work of reformation 'is ours and not your own'. He even intimidates MPs by telling them that 'you must expect to hear more frequently from us than ye have done'. However, there is no evidence in the other sources to support Source E's remarks about Parliament. Moreover, none of the sources offers evidence to support Source I's assertion that the Levellers 'spoke insolently' against 'the great officers of the army'.

In contrast, Sources E, F and G each support Source I's notion that the Levellers professed a 'great malice' against the Lords. Source E asserts that the Lords are an 'abuse', not having been chosen by 'the People'. Source F alleges that the Levellers will 'make every degree / To our royalty bow the knee'. Also, Source G insists that the Lords 'claimed many prerogatives' that removed them from 'common justice', a consequence of them being 'licensed in vice'.

Source I's accusation that the Levellers sought to level 'degrees of men' and establish 'equality' is supported by Source F's claim that the Levellers aimed to 'level the proud'. Source E makes no explicit claim to want to 'level', though that this was an objective is implied in the tone of the extract. However, Source G claims that the 'sober Levellers were never guilty' of wanting to level 'all estates and qualities'. Source H, produced by the Levellers themselves, is a clear statement that the Levellers did not seek a 'levelling of men's estates and making all things in common'.

In conclusion, the opinion expressed in Source I is only partially supported by the content of the other sources.

SOURCES

3. THE DEFEAT OF THE LEVELLERS

Source J: Extract from the Putney Debates, 29 October 1647.

Colonel Rainsborough: For really I think that the poorest he that is in England has a life to live as the greatest he; and therefore truly, sir, I think it is clear that every man that is to live under a government ought first by his own consent to put himself under that government; and I do think that the poorest man in England is not at all bound in a strict sense to that government that he has not had a voice to put himself under.

Ireton: I think it is no right at all ... No person has a right to an interest or share in the disposing or determining of the affairs of this kingdom and in choosing those that shall determine what laws we shall be ruled by here – no person has a right to this that has not a permanent fixed interest in this kingdom ... Those that choose the representers for the making of laws by which this state and kingdom are to be governed are the persons who, taken together, do comprehend the local interest of this kingdom, that is the persons in whom all land lies and those in corporations in whom all trading lies.

Source K: from the journal of Gilbert Mabbott.

[The author was clerk to John Rushworth, who in turn was secretary to Sir Thomas Fairfax. Here, Mabbott remarks upon the exchanges at the Putney Debates.]

The debate was prolonged so that some officers became angry with both sides saying, 'If we dispute here we are lost', and as one of them said, looking first at Cromwell and Ireton, and then at the agents Sexby and Wildman, 'both sides are obstinate and we shall be undone' ... Certainly it now seemed impossible that the Generals and Agitators could agree. And perhaps this is what Cromwell wants, a dividing of the Army so that he can rule.

Source L: Overton's *The Hunting of the Foxes*, March 1649.

[Produced shortly after the punishment of five soldiers for breaching new rules governing petitioning in the army.]

O Cromwell, O Ireton, how little time and success changed the honest shape of so many officers! . . . Was there ever a generation of men so apostate so false and so perjured as these? Did ever men pretend an higher degree of holiness, religion, and zeal to God and their country than these? . . . You shall scarce speak to Cromwell about anything, but he will lay his hand on his breast, elevate his eyes, and call God to record, he will weep, howl and repent, even while he doth smite you under the first rib.

Source M: an account by Lilburne after having faced the Council of State in April 1649 on a charge of treason.

After we were all come out . . . I laid my ear to the door and heard Lieutenant-General Cromwell (I am sure of it) very loud, thumping his fist upon the Council table till it rang again . . . speak in these very words, or to this effect: 'I tell you, Sir, you have no other way to deal with these men [the Levellers] but to break them in pieces. If you do not break them they will break you . . . Sir, I tell you again, you are necessitated to break them.'

Source N: Lilburne's *Epistle to the private soldiery of the army . . . especially those that hoped to plunder and destroy [those] traitorously defeated at Burford*, 15 May 1649.

You our fellow countrymen, the private soldiers of the Army, alone are the instrumental authors of your own slavery and ours. Therefore, as there is any bowels of men in you, any love to your native country, kindred, friends or relations, any sparks of conscience in you, any hopes of glory or immortality in you, or any pity, mercy, or compassion to an enslaved, undone, perishing, dying people: oh help! help! . . . be no more like brute beasts, to fight against us or our friends . . . to your own vassalage as well as ours.

Questions

1. What were the respective positions of authority of Cromwell and Ireton in March 1649? [2]
2. Read Sources J and L. Is there any evidence in J to support Overton's notion that many officers had once been of an 'honest shape'? [4]
*3. Read Sources K and M. Which of these do you consider more reliable as evidence of the character of Cromwell? [5]

4. With reference to their tone and language, which of the Sources M and N makes the most effective appeal to its audience? [6]
5. 'The Levellers failed because they did not succeed in winning the allegiance of members of the political nation.' To what extent do you agree? Refer to the sources and your own knowledge in your answer. [8]

Worked answer

*3. The historian should be cautious about accepting Lilburne's account. After all, he is a Leveller leader writing about a Grandee – most of whom became overtly antagonistic towards the Levellers. He is therefore predisposed to present Cromwell in an unflattering manner. Moreover, since the extract is undated it is possible that Lilburne was writing at some time after the collapse of the Leveller movement. If so, his purpose is probably to show that the Levellers failed not because of their own weaknesses but because of the duplicitous nature of their erstwhile allies, the Grandees. Finally, as the author himself admits, he is uncertain as to whether he has correctly recalled the exact words of Cromwell. Instead, he alleges only that Cromwell spoke words 'to this effect'.

As clerk to John Rushworth it seems likely that Mabbott will have been well informed of events. He will almost certainly have seen a large number of important documents. However, the account is undated. His assertion that Cromwell wanted a divided army 'so that he can rule' might be informed by the events of the 1650s, when Cromwell ruled as Lord Protector. Alternatively, this remark could be evidence of Mabbott having Leveller sympathies and, if so, it may therefore be his intention to suggest that the divisions in the army were the fault of Cromwell.

Both documents must be treated cautiously. They are perhaps reliable only as examples of Leveller opinion of Cromwell.

5

THE TRIAL AND EXECUTION OF KING CHARLES I AND THE CONSTITUTIONAL CONSEQUENCES, 1649–1653

BACKGROUND NARRATIVE

On 28 December 1647 Charles rejected Parliament's latest terms for settlement, the Four Bills. When it became apparent that the King had two days previously concluded an alliance known as the Engagement with a faction of the Scots, the Commons passed a Vote of No Addresses forbidding further negotiations with Charles. The effect on the New Model Army was even more dramatic, the soldiers vowing at a prayer meeting at Windsor Castle on 29 April to bring 'Charles Stuart, that man of blood' to account.[1]

Hoping to link up with a series of substantial risings in south Wales, East Anglia, Kent, Yorkshire and other smaller risings elsewhere, Hamilton, a leading Engager, led a Scottish force of ultimately about 20,000 into England on 8 July. However, Hamilton was no military man and his force was destroyed by Cromwell in a running battle around Preston (17–19 August). To army and Leveller disdain, most MPs, agitated by the programme of the radicals and unable to contemplate a settlement without the King, now repealed the Vote of No Addresses (24 August) and urgently resumed negotiations with Charles. If Charles, imprisoned in Carisbrooke Castle on the Isle of Wight since the previous November, acceded to the terms of the Treaty of Newport it appeared to the soldiers that many of their aims, as articulated in the Heads of the Proposals, would be put in jeopardy. Thus, to prevent any such settlement from going ahead, they purged Parliament of all those MPs who had voted to continue negotiations with Charles and others who had shown sympathy to the King or antipathy to the army. The ultimate consequence of Pride's Purge on 6 December 1648 was the trial and execution of the King, the latter event occurring on 30 January 1649. In the spring of 1649 legislation was enacted that formally abolished the monarchy and the House of Lords.

Until April 1653 the purged Parliament (known as the Rump) assumed supreme legislative power. However, three factors in particular meant that it did very little to meet the demands of its creator, the army. First, MPs were obliged instead to concentrate their energies upon securing the new regime from threats from the Levellers, Ireland, Scotland and latterly Holland. Second, the return of some moderate MPs to the Rump meant that its reforming impetus was blunted. Third, increasingly overwhelmed by the practical minutiae of day-to-day government, the Rump enacted very little legislation. Whereas 125 Acts had been passed in 1649 this number declined to only 44 in 1652. In these circumstances Cromwell was persuaded to dissolve the Rump of the Long Parliament on 20 April 1653. Its place was taken by a Nominated Assembly, comprising 139 'persons fearing God, and of approved fidelity and honesty' selected by the army officers.[2] However, on 12 December 1653 the moderate majority, increasingly frightened by the actions of the radicals in the Assembly, surrendered their power back to Cromwell.

ANALYSIS (1): WHAT CIRCUMSTANCES AND ARGUMENTS WERE DECISIVE IN BRINGING ABOUT THE TRIAL AND EXECUTION OF CHARLES I?

It is a somewhat easier task to suggest reasons why Charles I should not have been executed than to attempt an explanation of why he was.

For instance, the Whig interpretation that earlier events were leading inexorably to this climax has been disavowed by recent scholarship, as has the Marxist explanation that the regicide was induced by cumulative social and economic pressures.[3] Moreover, it is striking that both before and after the outbreak of the Civil War in 1642 doctrines of non-resistance and passive obedience were widely accepted, instilled by the twin notions of the 'divine right of kings' and the social and religious doctrine of the 'great chain of being'. Biblical texts such as Romans 13 warned that since 'the powers that be are ordained of God, whosoever therefore resisteth that power, resisteth the ordinance of God. And they that resist . . . shall receive to themselves damnation.' Disorder and rebellion were therefore as futile as they were sinful. It is little wonder that Henry Marten was (temporarily) expelled from the Commons in 1643 for arguing a case for a republic. It is also true that when the King was put on trial the Scots let it be known that they considered themselves bound by their Covenant to preserve monarchy. Thus, after Charles I's execution on 30 January 1649 some of the crowd rushed forward to dip their handkerchiefs in the royal blood, others to collect pocketfuls of earth from below the scaffold. One observer recorded that as the axe fell there was 'such a groan as I never heard before, and desire I may never hear again'.[4] Extraordinary events are usually the product of peculiar circumstances.

On 6 December 1648, under the auspices of Colonel Pride and his body of soldiers who had taken up position in the lobby of the Commons, the army arrested 45 MPs and prevented a further 186 from sitting. Besides these, a total of 86 withdrew in protest and a further 80 or so held aloof during December and January but returned in February 1649. Those whom the army permitted to continue to sit, and who chose to do so – a total of around only seventy MPs – in what became known as the Rump Parliament quickly set about effecting the arrangements for the trial of the King. It is inconceivable that this trial and the subsequent execution of Charles I would have occurred if the army had refrained from purging Parliament, an event to which they were driven by a number of factors: the machinations of Charles; the actions of Parliament; the leadership and impetus provided by Ireton (and latterly Cromwell); and the pressures brought about by a coalition formed in London between the Independents, religious separatists and the Levellers.

The King's decision to foment a Second Civil War by forming an alliance with a faction of the Scots according to the terms of the Engagement of 26 December 1647 did much both to harden and radicalise opinion against him.[5] Cromwell was moved to lament what he perceived to be an attempt 'to vassalize us to a foreign nation'.[6] Then, after a prayer meeting at Windsor that ended on 1 May 1648, the army resolved 'to call Charles Stuart, that man of blood, to an account for that blood he had shed, and mischief he had done to his utmost against the Lord's cause and people in these poor nations'.[7] Upon the efficient suppression of a series of provincial uprisings and the rout of Hamilton's army by Cromwell at Preston (17–19 August) – an occasion that Cromwell believed was 'nothing but the hand of God' – the soldiers expected Charles to be brought to justice and that this would be done by Parliament.[8]

Nor did this seem an unreasonable expectation. Upon learning that Charles had formed an Engagement with the Scots, Parliament's reaction had been initially similar to that of the army. After all, the Engagement had been signed at the same time as Charles had been contemplating Parliament's latest peace terms, the Four Bills.[9] Thus, to the majority of MPs, here was a duplicitous king who could not be trusted to abide by the terms of any settlement. 'Men who would have been willing to come to terms with him [thus] despaired of any constitutional arrangement in which he was to be a factor', observes S. R. Gardiner, 'and men who had long been alienated from him were irritated into active hostility'.[10] Consequently, on 3 January 1648 the Commons passed a Vote of No Addresses in which they resolved 'that they will make no further addresses or applications to the King' and that those who breached this order 'shall incur the penalties of high treason'.[11] However, as is usual in such circumstances, the unity that had existed among the anti-Royalist elements in the Second Civil War quickly evaporated upon the King's defeat and the old antagonism between Presbyterians and Independents once again came to the fore. On 24 August Parliament repealed the Vote of No Addresses and on 18 September reopened negotiations with Charles at Newport on the basis of the Newcastle Propositions. The Independents realised that henceforth they could probably only achieve their ambitions by force.

The soldiers too were coming to this conclusion. The army now had a reason to use force against Parliament not only because of the latter's softening of its position against a king whom the soldiers considered to be 'a man of blood', but because of a series of provocative actions by Parliament towards the army itself. Besides the steps taken towards disbanding the newly raised forces and the refusal to increase the military establishment by the 3,000 that Fairfax considered necessary to man the newly captured garrisons, Parliament continued its stubborn refusal to address the army's financial difficulties. As a result, according to Blair Worden (who minimises the influence of the Levellers' programme of reforms on the soldiers), 'the troops were evidently given to believe that a march on London would provide access to large sums of money stored in the city treasuries, and that the MPs who were to be imprisoned had been largely responsible for withholding their pay'.[12] Parliament further antagonised the army by appointing to the mastership of the armouries in the Tower and at Greenwich, Anthony Nicholl, a leading Presbyterian who had been in the forefront of moves against the army in 1647. Above all, when, on 20 November the army submitted to Parliament their Remonstrance of the Army demanding 'that the capital and grand author of our troubles, the person of the King . . . may be speedily brought to justice for the treason, blood and mischief he is guilty of', MPs chose to ignore the army's requests.[13] In the hope that their physical presence would persuade the MPs to do their bidding, the army once again occupied London (2 December), having already moved the person of the King from Newport to Hurst Castle (1 December). However, despite the presence of the military, the Commons voted on 5 December to continue their negotiations with Charles. Circumstances therefore forced the army either to purge (or perhaps dissolve) Parliament of those MPs who seemed determined to restore Charles at whatever cost or to accept that their war aims, as delineated in the Remonstrance and elsewhere, be thwarted.

It was unlikely that the army would have been able to effect the *coup d'état* of 6 December, and then go on to organise the trial and execution of the King, without the support of religious and political radicals in London. That the latter enjoyed substantial popular backing was evidenced by the 40,000 names that were attached to the Levellers' Humble Petition submitted to the Commons on 11 September.[14] Two days later, those who supported the Petition returned to Westminster in order to insist that the House consider the details of the Humble Petition before it came to terms with the King. H. N. Brailsford considers that this petition and demonstration 'cut a channel for the main current of revolutionary opinion in the country and swept the army into action'.[15] Indeed, at least seventeen other petitions supporting the Humble Petition of September reached Fairfax between October and December. Accordingly, Cromwell and Ireton reopened relations with the Leveller leaders. By mid-November it was agreed that a joint committee of four parliamentary (political) Independents, four London (religious) Independents, four army leaders and four Levellers should set about drafting a new version of the Agreement of the People as the basis for a constitutional settlement.

These moves to reconcile the Levellers' views of a settlement with, on the one hand, those of leading London and Parliamentarian radicals and, on the other hand, with both more moderate and more radical elements in the army would almost certainly not have occurred if it were not for the dynamic and dedicated leadership of Henry Ireton. He did much to build and maintain the radical coalition that was the necessary backcloth to the execution of the King. The author of the Solemn Engagement and other manifestos of the New Model Army including the Remonstrance of 1648, Ireton had grown determined to bring the King to trial and ultimately to execute him. In place of the increasingly diffident person of the Lord General Fairfax – who, through illness, real or imagined, was frequently absent from the decision-making process – Ireton eventually enjoyed the wholehearted support of his father-in-law, Oliver Cromwell. The latter, having been perhaps deliberately absent during Pride's Purge, was still arguing late in December that 'there was no policy in taking away [the King's] life'.[16] Yet shortly afterwards, having listened to Algernon Sidney's arguments against the validity of the court that was to try the King, Cromwell replied, 'I tell you we will cut off his head with the crown on it.'[17]

Cromwell's resolve to kill the King had been shaped by his conviction that he was submitting to God's will. 'Since the Providence of God hath cast this upon us', he is reported to have said, 'I cannot but submit to Providence.'[18] To Cromwell and others, it was now clear that since Charles was not prepared to make meaningful and sincere concessions in order to proceed with a settlement then settlement could only be had without him. As Essex had said of Strafford, 'stone dead hath no fellow'.[19]

Thus, on 6 January 1649 the Rump Parliament, acting as a mouth-piece for the army, passed an Act setting up the High Court of Justice that was to try Charles. It alleged that the King 'had a wicked design totally to subvert the ancient and fundamental laws and liberties of this nation and . . . that he [had] levied and maintained a cruel war in the land against Parliament'.[20] The Rump concluded that such activities amounted to High Treason, a necessary charge for those who wanted to kill the King because an act of treason carried the penalty of death. Yet it was palpably absurd to charge the King with treason because, from the time of its first statutory definition in 1352, this law held that the person guilty of that offence was one who 'compasses or imagines the death of our Lord the King', one who 'makes war against our said Lord the King in his Kingdom, or is an adherent of enemies to our Lord the King in the Kingdom'.[21]

To vindicate the trial and execution of the King it was therefore necessary to redefine treason. Thus, on 1 January 1649 Parliament declared that 'it is treason in the King of England . . . to levy war against the Parliament and Kingdom of England'.[22] Yet, such action also necessitated that the Rump Parliament press into further service those arguments that had already been used to justify resistance to Charles. The notion that the public safety was the highest law – *salus populi suprema lex* – was thus reinforced. Building on Henry Parker's theory that popular consent was the origin of government, and Leveller notions that provided a justification for republicanism, the case was made that Charles had abused the trust that was inherent to his position and that he had breached the laws of the land. It followed from this that the people, as represented in Parliament, were justified in calling him to account. Kings are 'subject to the Laws of the Land, and liable to Execution of death upon breach of that trust,' claimed the Leveller newspaper, the *Moderate*.[23] In order to assert yet further the validity of their actions, the Rump thus declared the sovereignty of Parliament, though 'Parliament' was now taken to refer to the Commons alone. On 4 January the Commons resolved that 'the people are, under God, the original of all just power; . . . that the Commons . . . have supreme power in this nation; and . . . that whatsoever is enacted and declared for law by the Commons in Parliament assembled has the force of law . . . although the consent of and concurrence of the King and House of Lords be not had thereunto'.[24] Meanwhile, Puritan preachers had for some time been at work, reciting sermons that quoted texts such as the passage on the curse of Meroz in the Book of Judges that justified resistance to an ungodly ruler and revising the established meaning of Romans, chapter 13.

However, few were convinced by such arguments. As the trial got under way, Lady Fairfax, the Lord General's wife, in response to the charge against Charles being read 'on the behalf of the Commons assembled in Parliament and the good people of England', cried out, 'It is a lie. Not half, nor a quarter of the people of England.'[25] Yet more damaging to the legitimacy of the court was Northumberland's assertion that he believed that 'not one in twenty of the people in England are yet satisfied whether the King did levy war first, or the Houses first against him; and, besides, if the King did levy war first, we have no law extant that can be produced to make it treason in him to do'.[26] Charles himself employed some of these points in order to justify his refusal to plead. For instance, he told the court that since they had 'never asked . . . the tenth man in the kingdom' they could make no claim to represent the will of the people.[27] For reasons such as these, only 59 of the 135 commissioners of the High Court signed the King's death warrant. The arguments of those who wished to remove the King thus appear to have been more divisive than they were decisive.

It was, of course, both circumstance and argument that led to Charles I being executed outside the Banqueting Hall on 30 January 1649. However, it is difficult to avoid the conclusion that the former played a more significant role than the latter and that, in the whole process, the pressure of events – as is so often the case – was ultimately more compelling than words.

Questions

1. 'Cruel necessity.' Is this a sufficient explanation for the execution of Charles I?
2. 'As long as he remained a factor in English politics, government by compromise was impossible.' Discuss this opinion of Charles I.

ANALYSIS (2): WHY COULD NEITHER THE RUMP NOR THE NOMINATED ASSEMBLY PROVIDE STABLE GOVERNMENT IN THE PERIOD 1649–1653?

Any regime that is instituted by an act of force, or in some other way denies the electorate an influence in deciding how the machinery of government is to be staffed, is unlikely to receive widespread popular support. The Rump Parliament (fathered in an act of violence by the army on 6 December 1648) and its successor, the Nominated Assembly (devised largely by the Fifth Monarchist Thomas Harrison, though it received much broader support among senior army officers and the Army Council), both rested on narrow bases of support from their inception. Their task of providing stable government was made more problematic because both regimes had to cope with the extraordinarily difficult legacy of the Civil Wars. It was an inauspicious beginning to the republican era.

Moreover, the republic was born out of negative rather than positive forces. Those who had supported the regicide had done so more because they wished to destroy Charles I, that 'man of blood', rather than from any ideological preference for republican government. That this was the case is evidenced by the very halting way in which the new regime was established, which is perhaps not surprising considering that only about 15 per cent of the membership of the Rump can be labelled as active revolutionaries. During the first three months of the regime the average attendance in the Commons was only 56 out of about 211.[28] This helps to explain why it was not until 17 and 19 March that Acts were passed to abolish formally the monarchy and House of Lords respectively, though the Commons had voted as early as 6 and 7 February to implement this course of action. As late as 19 May England was declared to be 'a Commonwealth and Free State'. In January 1650, acting more from fear than ideological enthusiasm, the Rump continued to betray its insecurity by demanding the allegiance of all adult males of eighteen years and over. It obliged them to take an Engagement that they would be 'true and faithful to the Commonwealth of England, as it is now established'.[29] Derek Hirst believes this was 'a major political mistake. In demanding more than mere passive acquiescence as the warrant for full citizenship it concentrated attention on the propriety of allegiance to usurpers and on the degree to which other oaths were being breached.'[30] Indeed, only 19 of the 41 who sat on the Council of State took the Engagement, indicating, as Blair Worden has observed, that the Rump suffered from an 'absence among those whom the revolution brought to power of a positive and clearly defined ideology'.[31]

In contrast to the Rump, recent research has proved that the Nominated Assembly, driven forward by a knot of radicals, evinced a sense of direction and purpose.[32] Yet, the 139 'persons fearing God, and of approved fidelity and honesty' who assumed their seats for the opening session on 4 July 1653 could never hope to compel widespread allegiance.[33] Based on the ancient Jewish Sanhedrin or assembly of saints, these men – nominated by the separatist congregations and army officers (though the overwhelming majority probably by the latter) – seem to have been expected to inculcate a godliness in the general population, which in turn would lead the latter to believe that their best interests were served by a republic. Only when that understanding had been reached could a general election be held. Such reasoning amounted to 'a candid admission that the republican regime rested upon no more than minority support in the country as a whole'.[34]

Even more destabilising than an absence of positive support was the fact that the republic was assaulted by its detractors from both the left and right. The first to strike were the Levellers, whose principles had been so betrayed by the unrepresentative nature of the Rump and the unconstitutionality of its proceedings. In the spring of 1649 several regiments based in the south of England mutinied, only to be efficiently put down at Burford by Cromwell and Fairfax on 14–15 May. Meanwhile, the anarchy of the war years had unleashed yet more radical left-wing groups such as the Diggers. These 'True Levellers' believed in common ownership of land and were led by Gerrard Winstanley.

Numbering no more than several hundred, they never posed a direct threat to the regime, though to many propertied observers their emergence probably did much to encourage a sympathy with the old monarchical form of government. This was certainly the effect of sectarian groups such as the Fifth Monarchists and Muggletonians, millenarian elements who perceived the regicide as a prelude to the Second Coming of Christ. Drawing their support from the lower orders of society and emphasising the power of the individual spirit, they created deep concern among property owners. The Ranters – though there is a fierce debate about whether they actually existed or were created by the political establishment merely to frighten the elite and taint all radical groups – who seem to have believed that 'sin hath its conception only in the imagination', produced a similar effect.[35] By far the most numerous of these groups were the Quakers. Stressing the notion of an 'inner light' existing within the soul – the recognition of which would bring divine redemption – the Quakers refused to swear oaths, pay tithes or remove their hats in the presence of anyone. To property-owning contemporaries, these were Levelling tendencies indeed and, as such, had to be abhorred.

An even more substantial threat to the republic came from the right. Those MPs arrested or secluded by Pride formed a hard core of resentment, though the political leadership of the Presbyterians was already broken and demoralised – Denzil Holles, for example, having fled to France. By far the greatest danger came from outside England. In 1649 Ireland was still in revolt. Since there appeared every likelihood that Charles Stuart would put himself at the head of the rebellious forces it became necessary for the republic to take pre-emptive action. Cromwell was therefore sent to Ireland by the Rump and, benefiting from Colonel Michael Jones's victory at Rathmines on 2 August, effectively quelled the rebellion by the end of the year. However, in the meantime, Charles Stuart, after being proclaimed as King Charles II by the Scots and having signed the Covenants on 23 June 1650, formed an alliance with that nation. Yet the Scottish military effort to restore Charles to his English throne – sometimes known as the Third Civil War – was thwarted by Cromwell, initially at Dunbar on 3 September 1650 and then finally at Worcester exactly one year later.

Paradoxically, the extinguishing of these threats revealed new dangers to the regime. First, the army, previously occupied on its campaigns, was now possessed of a leisure that enabled it to monitor more carefully the Rump's progress towards effecting a moral and godly reformation. It did not like what it saw. For instance, in terms of religion, although the Rump had passed a Toleration Act on

27 October 1650, its terms – largely because of the effect of the appearance of the various sects – were such that to label it as an Act providing toleration is to mislead. What it gave with one hand it took with the other. Moreover, despite the appointment of a commission led by Matthew Hale to reform the law, none of its recommendations was implemented. Nor was the amount of legislation passed by the Rump impressive, falling from 152 Acts in 1649 to only 51 in 1652. Above all, though it had resolved in September 1651 to dissolve itself no later than 3 November 1654, there was little indication that MPs were preparing to stand down. The Rump's lethargy reignited the army's political agenda, which in turn compromised the authority of that assembly. In the last resort, the civilian leaders of the republic were 'sitting on bayonets'.[36] Second, the various threats to the continued existence of the new regime – including a war against the Dutch that broke out in 1652 – had made it necessary to enlarge the size of the army, though it had been contracted to a total of 31,500 in England and Wales by December 1652. Even so, the costs of maintaining such a force – £111,000 per month – prevented the divisions that had emerged during the Civil Wars from being healed and settled. The Rump voted on 4 December 1652 that the monthly assessment be raised from £90,000 to the unprecedented level of £120,000. In this way resentment at the lack of a peace dividend translated into resentment of the regime. Life under a monarchy had been a cheaper option.

Perhaps the greatest source of both stability and instability during this period was Oliver Cromwell himself. He was an increasingly influential politician, his position enhanced by the fact that he had become Lord General in June 1650 after Fairfax declined to lead the campaign against the Scots. Yet he seems to have been suffering from what Blair Worden has diagnosed as 'ideological schizophrenia'.[37] Thus, the man who had eventually become resolute in his determination to kill the King was also capable, as early as 1651, of wondering 'what if a man should take upon him to be a king?'[38] Equally, though he told his audience at the Army Council debates in Reading on 16 July 1647 'that [although] we have got things of the Parliament by force, and we know what it is to have that stain lie upon us', on 20 April 1653 he entered the Commons accompanied by musketeers and forcibly dissolved the Rump.[39] This kaleidoscopic nature of Cromwell's personality prevented him from providing sustained, assured leadership. Having exchanged the decisiveness of the battlefield for the fog of politics, Cromwell seems too often to have been waiting for a sign from God of what to do – but Providence did not always provide. Cromwell himself concluded that the failure of the Nominated Assembly was 'a story of my own weakness and folly'.[40] 'Without direction', observes Toby Barnard, 'the Barebones Parliament [Nominated Assembly] tended to go where the radicals blew.'[41]

Above all, Cromwell's twin aims of effecting godly reformation and constitutional propriety were probably mutually exclusive given the prevailing circumstances. Ironically, though he lamented the lack of radical thrust by the Rump, it was partly the result of his own action by inviting back to the Commons a number of those MPs either excluded by Pride or who had stayed away in the immediate aftermath of the purge and trial and execution of the King, thus blunting the reforming agenda of the Rump. Arguably, Cromwell might have achieved either of his aims fairly easily but by attempting to achieve both simultaneously he induced a fateful instability into the affairs of the republic. In December 1653, when the members of the Nominated Parliament resigned their powers back to Cromwell, England was no more settled than at any time since the regicide.

Stable government in all early modern societies was somewhat elusive. That it proved unattainable in England given the unique nature of the circumstances of 1649–1653 is thus perhaps not surprising. On the other hand, considering that the republic was created by the actions of a few, it is perhaps surprising that there was not greater political turmoil during this period.

Questions

1. How successful was the Commonwealth in domestic affairs?
2. 'Destined to fail from the very start.' Discuss this opinion of the Rump and Nominated Parliaments.

SOURCES

1. THE EXECUTION OF CHARLES I

Source A: the charge that was read to the King, 23 January 1649.

Charles Stuart, King of England, you are accused on the behalf of the Commons of England of divers high crimes and treasons.

Source B: a regicide justifying himself ten years after the execution.

It is impossible that any man should delight in a man of so much blood as the King was . . . He was seven or eight times sent to with propositions, and would not yield . . . So long as he was above ground, in view, there were daily revoltings among the army, and risings in all places; creating us all mischief, more than a thousand kings could do us good. It was impossible to continue him alive.

Source C: an account by John Downes, after the Restoration, when he was about to stand trial for his part in the regicide.

The President . . . commanded the clerk to read the sentence. God knows I lie not, my heart was ready to burst within me. [Since I was] sitting on the seat next to Cromwell, he perceived some discomposure in me, and turned to me and said, 'What ails thee? Art thou mad? Canst thou not sit still and be quiet?' I answered 'Quiet! No Sir, I cannot be quiet', and then . . . I stood up and . . . said: 'My Lord President, I am not satisfied to give my consent to this sentence . . . And as this relation shows, I am but a weak and imprudent man, yet I did what I could. I did my best, I could do no more. I was single, I was alone; only I ought not to have been there at all.

Source D: from Clarendon's _History_.

The next day [28 January 1649] after the horrid sentence was pronounced [Ingoldsby went to the Painted Chamber where he saw Cromwell and others] assembled to sign the warrant for his Majesty's death. As soon as Cromwell's eyes were upon him, he ran to him, and taking him by the hand, drew him by force to the table and said . . . he should now sign that paper as well as they. Which [Ingoldsby], seeing what it was, refused with great passion . . . But Cromwell and others held him by violence; and Cromwell, with a loud laughter, taking his hand in his, and putting the pen between his fingers, with his own hand wrote Richard Ingoldsby, he making all the resistance he could.

Source E: from the _Memoirs of the Life of Colonel Hutchinson_, as written by his widow, Lucy.

Some of [the regicides] afterwards, for excuse, belied themselves, and said they were under the awe of the army, and overpersuaded by Cromwell and the like. But it is certain that all men herein were left to their free liberty of acting, neither persuaded nor compelled . . . [In 1660], when it came to Ingoldsby's turn, he, with many tears, professed his repentance for that murder, and told a false tale how Cromwell held his hand and forced him to subscribe the sentence.

Source F: Figure 1: a contemporary painting of Charles's execution by the Dutch artist Weesop.

Source F: Figure 1: *The Execution of Charles I*, by Weesop. By permission of the Earl of Rosebery and the Scottish National Portrait Gallery

Questions

1. Read Source B. (i) Give two examples of the 'propositions' that were sent to Charles.
   (ii) Comment upon the phrase 'risings in all places'. [4]
2. Read Sources B and C. With reference to the content and provenance of these sources and your own knowledge, which do you find the more convincing as an explanation for these men's participation in the trial of Charles I? Explain your answer. [4]
3. Either:
   In what ways does the artist of Source F betray his bias?; or
   In what ways would Source A be of use to the historian? [3]
4. Compare Sources D and E. How might you account for the differences between these sources? [6]
*5. 'Overpersuaded by Cromwell and the like.' Use these sources and your own knowledge to assess whether this is a sufficient explanation for the killing of Charles I. [8]

Worked answer

*5. Sources C and D create an impression that Cromwell was indeed the driving force behind the regicide, suggesting to Downes that he was 'mad' when the latter felt 'some discomposure' about proceeding with the trial of Charles. Similarly, the author of Source D alleges that Cromwell 'drew [Ingoldsby] by force to the table', and, along with others, 'held him by violence' and forced him to sign the King's death warrant. This notion that men were coerced by the army seems to be supported by Source E's acknowledgement that some of the regicides claim to have been 'overpersuaded by Cromwell and the like'. However, this author goes on to insist that 'it is certain' that those who signed the King's death warrant were 'neither persuaded or compelled' to do so and that Ingoldsby's story was 'a false tale'. It is certainly the case that the author of Source B gives no inkling that he signed the death warrant because he was intimidated by Cromwell and the army. Instead, he argues that Charles I's intransigence – 'he was seven or eight times sent to with propositions' – meant that 'it was impossible to continue him alive'.

Very few had been 'overpersuaded' to kill the King, only 59 of the 135 members of the High Court having signed Charles's death warrant. There was no popular support for the regicide, as demonstrated by the overwhelming grief that afflicted those who witnessed the execution outside the Banqueting House on 30 January 1649 (Source F). One observer noted that as the King's head was severed from his neck there was 'such a groan as I never heard before'. The regicide was instead the act of a determined military minority, covering its tracks by claiming to be acting in the name of the Commons (Source A). In April 1648 the army had declared Charles 'a man of blood' and on 20 November had presented a Remonstrance to Parliament, demanding that Charles, 'the capital and grand author of all our troubles', be brought to justice. When it appeared that Parliament was bent on ignoring the wishes of the army the soldiers purged the Commons of its enemies. Those who remained (the Independents) were the natural allies of the army and needed little persuading to acquiesce in the killing of the King. Nor is it true that Cromwell played a key role in all of this, resolving only late in the day to 'cut off [the King's head] with the crown on it'. Not only had Cromwell been absent from London when the army purged Parliament (6 December 1648) but in that month he was still arguing that 'there was no policy in taking away [the King's] life'.

Despite the evidence of Sources C and D the regicide was therefore less the result of a group of men 'overpersuaded by Cromwell and the like' than the inevitable outcome of an army that had lost its patience with its king.

6

THE PROTECTORATE OF OLIVER CROMWELL, 1653–1658

BACKGROUND NARRATIVE

On 16 December 1653 Oliver Cromwell was installed as Lord Protector according to the terms of the Instrument of Government, a written constitution prepared by John Lambert and the Council of Officers, perhaps in consultation with several civilian politicians. It permitted Cromwell and his Council to rule by ordinance until 3 September 1654 when he was obliged to meet with a Parliament. However, Cromwell's hopes that Parliament would set about 'healing and settling' the nation were quickly dashed. Instead MPs criticised the Instrument, speaker after speaker attacking one of the key aspects of the new constitution – the sharing of power between a single person and Parliament. Thus, in order to identify his enemies, Cromwell forced MPs on 12 September either to sign a Recognition – whereby they demonstrated their assent to the principle of a single person and Parliament – or to withdraw from Westminster. Of the 460 MPs elected to the First Protectorate Parliament about one hundred chose the latter course, though Parliament continued to function after 12 September. Indeed, a range of Bills was considered, but most work focused on a Government Bill designed to replace the Instrument. Although Cromwell welcomed the prospect of a new parliamentary constitution, there were aspects of the evolving Government Bill that he found unacceptable, prompting him to dissolve Parliament on 22 January 1655 – the earliest occasion he was able to do so according to the Instrument.

A Royalist rebellion led by Penruddock in the spring of 1655 was one of the reasons why Cromwell divided England into ten (later eleven) military districts, each of which was presided over by a major-general. Yet their influence was patchy and certainly diminishing even before the Second Protectorate Parliament, which first met on 17 September 1656, voted in January 1657 to end the collection of the decimation tax, the levy on Royalists that financed the major-generals experiment. A desire for supply had prompted Cromwell to call the Second Parliament, the first session of which proved considerably more successful than its predecessor – at least in part because it had been heavily purged by the Council before it met. However, MPs' vicious treatment of the Quaker James Naylor persuaded Cromwell that the single-chamber Parliament would benefit from the check of an upper house. Moreover, since Cromwell was now more concerned than ever for his government to acquire some constitutional legitimacy he accepted the civilian-devised Humble Petition and Advice, though without the position of king, on 25 May 1657. A month later (26 June) he was reinstalled as Lord Protector with many of the trappings of monarchy.

In the second session of Cromwell's Second Parliament (20 January–4 February 1658) the Protectorate once again ran into difficulties. The excluded members returned and vented their anger at their earlier treatment and at what they perceived to be the apostasy of Oliver Cromwell, his betrayal of the Good Old Cause. In other words, they resented Cromwell's apparent abandonment of everything for which he and his supporters had fought since 1642 – including, latterly, the republican ideals articulated in 1648/9 – in return for his elevation as 'a king in all but name'. By the time of his death on 3 September 1658 he was thus reviled alike by the republicans and Royalists, the former believing him to be a traitor and the latter seeing him as a usurper.

ANALYSIS: IS IT POSSIBLE TO DESCRIBE THE PROTECTORATE OF OLIVER CROMWELL AS A MILITARY DICTATORSHIP?

Ever since his own time the popular impression of Lord Protector Oliver Cromwell has been that of a despotic autocrat, an 'absolute Lord and Tyrant'.[1] The Restoration unleashed a flood of such opinion, one author choosing to call his subject 'The English Devil'. Another, in a tract published in 1682, concluded that the Protectorate had been a time of 'Tyranny, Oppression and Injustice' perpetrated by Cromwell, who 'ruled by himself with greater power and more absolute Sway than ever any Monarch of England did'.[2] Moving forward in time, the emergence of the European dictatorships of the twentieth century led, perhaps inevitably, to comparisons between, on the one hand, Oliver Cromwell, and, on the other, Hitler, Mussolini and Stalin. For instance, W. C. Abbott, in his *Writings and Speeches of Oliver Cromwell*, drew parallels between his subject and Hitler.[3] Meanwhile, in the *Saturday Review* in 1934, Clive Rattigan described Cromwell as 'a 17th-century Hitler–Mussolini, rolled into one'.[4] More generally, H. N. Brailsford, writing in the 1960s, believed that the Protectorate amounted to 'a totalitarian dictatorship' and that 'the efficient police state which Thurloe constructed was as highly centralised as any of the totalitarian regimes of our own century'.[5] However, the most recent research has concluded that 'the picture of Cromwell as an all-powerful, unfettered autocrat who knew no constitutional restraints, and of his Council as a politically impotent façade, overawed, manipulated or ignored by a tyrannical Protector, is fundamentally inaccurate'.[6]

Such is the nature of Cromwell's character and career that he has been described at once as 'one of the most notorious tyrants and usurpers that the world ever beheld' and 'a great champion for the liberties of the nation'.[7] The provision of an objective assessment of the nature of Cromwell's Protectorate is therefore a difficult task, and the notion of whether it amounted to a dictatorship is made problematic because of differing opinions as to what defines that term. Nevertheless, most commentators would agree that any such government must possess an ideology that imbues the dictator with a claim to total obedience. In addition, it has been asserted that a dictatorship is:

> a regime that acknowledges no constitutional restraints, that openly subordinates the rights of the individual to the interests of the state, that denies or at least compromises the rule of law because the law lies ultimately in the dictator's will, that commands absolutely whatever means of coercion – armed forces, police, bureaucracy,

judiciary – the state possesses, and that can control such means of persuasion and propaganda as the current technology affords.[8]

Using this definition as a benchmark, it is clear that there was an element of, if not dictatorship, then heavy-handedness during the Protectorate of Oliver Cromwell.

In a number of respects each of the two written constitutions by which Cromwell was elevated to the position of Lord Protector imbued him with significant constitutional powers. The Instrument of Government, devised by John Lambert and accepted by the Council of Officers in December 1653, appointed Cromwell for life. There was no provision for forcible dismissal or voluntary resignation. He could be removed only by death. All magistracy and honours were 'derived' from the Lord Protector. He also possessed significant powers of pardon, could delay and veto parliamentary Bills, was empowered to rule by ordinance until the First Protectorate Parliament met and was able to dissolve Parliament after a period of only five months. Indeed, it was constitutionally legitimate for the Lord Protector to rule without a Parliament for up to thirty-one months in any thirty-six-month period. The Instrument also provided a financial settlement from which the army was to be maintained and that was not subject to parliamentary interference.[9] The civilian-devised constitution that Cromwell finally accepted in May 1657, the Humble Petition and Advice – and the Additional Petition – modified a number of these provisions in ways that generally enhanced the role of Parliament.[10] Nevertheless, the chief executive was now provided with the constitutional ability to name his successor, to declare war and make peace, to nominate the founder members of both the 'Other House' and, initially, the Privy Council. This latter was potentially particularly significant because Cromwell continued to be obliged to dispose the armed forces in the intervals of Parliament 'by the advice of the Council'. The Humble Petition also ensured generous financial provision for the army and navy – £1 million per annum. The powers to pardon offences, dissolve Parliament and veto legislation were not mentioned in the Humble and Additional petitions 'but presumably were vested in the Protector'.[11]

Nevertheless, it remains true that the majority of the terms of the constitutions meant that the Lord Protector was more restricted than a monarch operating with a Privy Council and Parliament. Yet theory was different from practice and the position of Lord Protector in the 1650s was unique. With no precedent to guide his behaviour, and perhaps anticipating occasions when the meaning of the constitutions would be open to debate – as Whitelocke observed, the title of King was grounded 'in all the ancient foundations of the laws of England' – it may be suggested that Cromwell declined the offer of the Crown because he realised that he had more (potential) power as Lord Protector.[12] In any case, as Lord General he possessed the means to coerce popular opinion. Indeed, by the end of 1654 the army totalled about 53,000 in all three kingdoms, 23,000 more than the number stipulated by the Instrument of Government. Cromwell 'had reserves of power', notes Peter Gaunt, 'which elevated him far above paper constitutions'.[13]

In addition to the power inherent in his position, Cromwell's personality appears to have had a dictatorial bent. 'Necessity hath no law,' he insisted to the First Protectorate Parliament on 12 September 1654.[14] 'If nothing should be done but what is according to the law,' said Cromwell in September 1656, 'the throat of the nation may be cut till we send for some to make a law.'[15] 'Tell [Cromwell] of Magna Carta,' reported the vitriolic *English Devil*, '[and] he would lay his hand on his sword and cry Magna Farta.'[16] Ominously, the Lord Protector let it be known that he believed that there could be occasions when 'the Supreme Magistrate' should not be 'tied up to the ordinary rules'.[17] It is thus of little surprise to learn that 1655–1656 has been called an 'era of petty tyranny', a period in which Cromwell became increasingly intolerant of attacks upon his authority according to the terms of the Instrument of Government.[18] For example, when two judges who had been sent to York to preside over the trials of Royalist insurgents in that region questioned the validity of the treason ordinance of 1654 they were called before the Council and dismissed from their posts on 3 May 1655. Then, three lawyers acting on behalf of a city merchant named Cony – imprisoned because he refused to pay customs on the basis that they lacked the authority of an Act of Parliament – found themselves incarcerated for arguing for his release and only regained their freedom (as did Cony) when they acknowledged their offence. The Chief Justice Henry Rolle sympathised with their plight and was duly called before the Council. Anticipating his dismissal, Rolle chose to resign on 7 June. On the previous day two Commissioners of the Great Seal – Whitelocke and Widdrington – had already resigned rather than implement a protectoral ordinance for the Reformation of Chancery. Finally, in August Sir Peter Wentworth was summoned before the Council for refusing to pay the assessment on the basis that it was not validated by law and was allowed to go free only when he had submitted. Even more indicative of the dictatorial tendency of the Lord Protector was the fate of Robert Overton, imprisoned by Cromwell for more than four years on suspicion of inducing a conspiracy in the army.

To many, it must have seemed that the 'ordinary rules' were being further disturbed when, in August 1655 – following on from a scheme that had been in operation under Desborough in the south-west in the early part of 1655 – England and Wales were divided into ten (later eleven) military districts. Each was placed under the command of a major-general whose task it was to raise a new militia in each county financed by a tax of one-tenth on the estates of known Royalists, the so-called decimation tax. The exactions imposed upon the Royalists prompted S. R. Gardiner to remark that 'every one of these orders frankly relinquished the domain of law'.[19] Indeed, they struck directly at the Act of Oblivion of 1652. In October 1655 the major-generals received specific instructions. Amongst other things, these demanded that they 'endeavour the suppressing [of] all tumults, insurrections, rebellions or other unlawful assemblies', maintain 'a strict eye upon the conversation and carriage of all disaffected persons' and ensure that the licences of certain ale houses 'be called in and suppressed'.[20] On paper at least, this appears to have been an extraordinary invasion of local affairs by central government. Meanwhile, Cromwell issued orders that the existing laws governing the press should be put into effect and stipulated that no one was to print 'books of news . . . unless authorised by us or our Council or licensed by those appointed thereto'.[21] Indeed, until September 1655 a total of eight weekly newspapers were available on the bookstalls but thereafter only the government-controlled *Mercurius Politicus* and *Publick Intelligencer* were permitted.

However, it is difficult to sustain this picture of Cromwell as a military dictator. Many of the instances cited above are newsworthy precisely because they are exceptions to the general tenor of government under Cromwell's Protectorate. Moreover, apart from the army, Cromwell lacked the apparatus that would have enabled him to act as a dictator. He possessed no police force or salaried bureaucracy that he could employ to enforce his will. Even some of the major-generals proved largely ineffectual. Instead, government in both the centre and the localities remained dependent upon the goodwill of the political nation. As the Stuart kings James I and Charles I had been aware, by far the greatest means of persuasion and propaganda possessed by an early modern ruler was through control of the Church. Yet Cromwell presided over the collapse of the State Church. Episcopacy had been abolished in 1646 and both of the written constitutions enshrined the principle of liberty to (Protestant) tender consciences.

Cromwell himself spoke of how the constitutions restricted his room for manoeuvre. For instance, he asserted that the Instrument 'limited me and bound my hands to act nothing to the prejudice of the nations without consent of a Council until the Parliament met'.[22] Clause after clause in both the Instrument and Humble Petition obliged the Lord Protector to govern 'by consent of Parliament', which he was obliged to call at least once every three years and permit to sit for at least five months, and, in the intervals of Parliament, by 'the major part of the Council'. Both constitutions stipulated that he seek Parliament's approval for appointments to the higher offices of state and vetted his choice of councillors. In the spring of 1657 Cromwell lamented the restrictive aspects of the Instrument. 'I was a child in its swaddling clouts,' he said. 'I cannot transgress by the Government. I can do nothing but in ordination with the Council.'[23] Of course, the historian must be cautious about accepting such remarks at their face value for Cromwell may have been attempting simply to justify his shortcomings. Yet it remains true that he only rarely exceeded the powers given him under the constitutions. Though it would be difficult to assert that the test (which Cromwell backed and probably even initiated) imposed upon the First Protectorate Parliament effectively excluding many MPs from 12 September 1654 was in accordance with the terms of the Instrument of Government, it seems that Cromwell objected to the pre-session exclusions of September 1656, being unhappy at the way in which the Council was manipulating the Instrument. In general it is clear that he sought Parliament's advice and consent where required to do so.

Cromwell's attitude to the law appears to have been equally conservative and there is no doubt that he took seriously his protectoral oath 'to govern these nations according to the laws, statutes and customs thereof'.[24] For instance, though there was a growing fear that juries might not convict – an outcome that could be avoided by erecting High Courts of Justice where both judge and jury were replaced by nominated commissioners – only two High Courts of Justice were instituted throughout the Protectorate, whereas there had been five such during the Commonwealth period, 1649–1653. Torture was not used at all after 1653, though its use had been ordered by Charles I as recently as 1640. Under Cromwell's Protectorate no one was executed for any political offence short of high treason. Moreover, of the leading participants of the failed Royalist rising led by Penruddock in March 1655, though thirty-nine were convicted of treason by a jury, less than half that number were executed while the others were transported to Barbados. Austin Woolrych has pointed out that their treatment was thus far more lenient than that which was meted out to the English rebels of 1569 and 1685.[25] Considering how frequently the regime was attacked, both by the pen and from the pulpit, it is also notable how infrequent was the imprisonment of dissidents and how late in the day the censorship orders occurred. Despite its difficulties, the regime allowed the system of common law to continue to function, apart from at a local level during the regime of the major-generals.

Yet recent research has suggested that 'the establishment of the major-generals marked much less of a break than has generally been supposed; it brought a difference in degree rather than in kind'.[26] It is now clear that the inauguration of the major-generals was not an experiment in centralisation. Rather they were 'bolted on to' the existing structures of local government. Nor were they instituted in order to erect some sort of police state but rather, by establishing a new militia financed by Royalists, Cromwell hoped they would allow him ultimately to reduce the size of the standing army that in turn would lead to a reduction in the assessment and thus advance prospects for healing and settling the nation. In any case the experiment proved largely ineffective and was short-lived. G. E Aylmer argues that the major-generals were of little import after September 1656, while Anthony Fletcher believes that they had passed their peak as early as May 1656.[27] More generally, the army intruded very little upon local government. Austin Woolrych has estimated that the ratio of military to civilian JPs available at any one time in the 1650s was about one in thirty, 'a rather mild threat to civil liberties'.[28] Other county-based commissions had similarly few army representatives. The Commission for the Ejectors, established by ordinance in August 1654 to expel ministers and schoolmasters who, among other things, were regarded as being 'scandalous in their lives and conversations', had a ratio of about one officer to every seventeen civilian Ejectors.[29] Meanwhile, on the county commissions responsible for the collection of the assessment about one commissioner in every fifty was an officer. Unlike some European countries, tax was not collected at sword point.

Nor was it the case that the affairs of state at the centre were dominated by the military. Of the eighteen councillors who had been appointed by June 1654, ten were civilians and only four – Lambert, Desborough, Fleetwood and Skippon – were unarguably regular officers. Of the Commission of Triers based in London – those who were responsible for the approbation of ministers – just two of the thirty-eight were army officers. It is also notable that the only Commissioners of the Treasury with any military links were Sydenham and Montague and that the Commissioners of the Great Seal were all lawyers who were unconnected with the army. Moreover, the standing army had a less intimidating presence, at least in England, than at first appears to be the case. Of its total strength of more than 50,000 in December 1654, only 11,000 soldiers were stationed in England, a total that was at least 2,000 fewer than the Rump had been maintaining in 1652. By July 1657 the military establishment in England was about 13,500, a slight increase that was indicative not of an embellishment of a military regime but merely the result of the withdrawal of troops from Scotland as that country became more peaceful. Moreover, as a proportion of the population of England and Wales (about 5 million in the mid-seventeenth century), a military establishment of 13,500 was not particularly great. Indeed, in contemporary European terms it was insignificant. It is also worth noting that in 1688 James II had an army of about 30,000 and, as Austin Woolrych has observed, 'if forces of that size could not save an anointed king from deposition, it is worth asking how much of a military dictatorship could be sustained by less than a third as many in Cromwell's England'.[30]

Above all, it is impossible to perceive Cromwell as being driven forward by an ideology that necessitated the formation of a dictatorship, even if that had been possible given the circumstances of the time. Instead, he was much more concerned to provide liberty to tender consciences and to 'heal and settle' the nation. To this end, he desired that the authority of government should run in the old channels as far as possible, with the exception that monarchy should not be resurrected – not because he himself might yet enjoy more power as Lord Protector, but because monarchy was an institution against which God had judged. 'I would not seek to set up that that providence hath destroyed and laid in the dust,' said Cromwell, 'and I would not build Jericho again.'[31] Time and again he appears fearful of the authority that he possessed, an impression bolstered by Peter Gaunt's argument that Cromwell was 'probably the driving force' behind at least two of the restrictive clauses – that is, clauses that limited the powers of the Protector – in the Additional Petition and Advice.[32]

Cromwell frequently insisted that he had 'no title to the government of these nations but what was taken up in a case of necessity [and that he would not seek] the continuance of [his] power or place, either under one title or another'.[33] Yet, it is also true that Cromwell, secure in the knowledge that his authority rested ultimately on army backing, acted with a certain heavy-handedness when he saw his hopes for settlement and reformation jeopardised by events like Penruddock's rebellion or when those in authority questioned the constitutional basis of the regime. He was, then, perhaps both a 'good constable' and, more occasionally, a reluctant dictator.

Questions

1. Is it possible to describe Lord Protector Oliver Cromwell as a 'reluctant dictator'?
2. 'The character of the Lord Protector and the limitations of the written constitutions of the 1650s are sufficient evidence that Oliver Cromwell could never have established a military dictatorship.' Discuss.

SOURCES

1. CROMWELL'S AIMS

Source A: from Cromwell's speech to the First Protectorate Parliament, 4 September 1654.

That which I judge to be the end of your meeting, the great end . . . [is] healing and settling.

Source B: from Cromwell's speech to the First Protectorate Parliament, 4 September 1654.

[What were] the ranks and orders of men whereby England had been known for hundreds of years? A nobleman, a gentleman, a yeoman; the distinction of these, that is a good interest of the nation, and a great one!

Source C: from Cromwell's letter to the County Committee of Suffolk, 29 August 1643.

If you choose godly, honest men to be captains of horse, honest men will follow them . . . I had rather have a plain russet-coated captain that knows what he fights for, and loves what he knows, than that which you call a gentleman and is nothing else. I honour a gentleman that is so indeed.

Source D: from Cromwell's speech to the First Protectorate Parliament, 12 September 1654.

Some things are fundamentals . . . The government by a single person and Parliament is a fundamental . . . That Parliaments should not make themselves perpetual, is a fundamental . . . Is not liberty of conscience in religion a fundamental? . . . It ought to be so. Another fundamental which I had forgotten is the militia . . . That it should be well and equally placed is very necessary. For, put the absolute power of the militia into the hands of one Person – without a check, what doth it serve? On the other hand [...] what check is there upon your Perpetual Parliaments if the Government be wholly stripped of this of the militia?

Source E: Cromwell at the Putney Debates, 28 October–1 November 1647.

They [the people] may have some jealousies and apprehensions that we [himself] are wedded and glued to forms of government... You will find that we are far from being so particularly engaged.

Source F: from the Quaker George Fox's *Journal*, published in 1694.

At [the Battle of Dunbar Cromwell] had promised to the Lord that if He gave him the victory over his enemies he would take away tithes, etc., or else let him be rolled into his grave with infamy.

Source G: Cromwell to the Second Protectorate Parliament, 17 September 1656.

For my part I should think I were very treacherous if I should take away tithes till I see the legislative power to settle maintenance to them [church ministers] another way.

Source H: from Cromwell's speech to the Second Protectorate Parliament, 17 September 1656.

I say... that the liberty... of this nation depends upon reformation, to make it a shame to see men to be bold in sin and profaneness.

Source I: from Cromwell's letter to William Lenthall, Speaker of the Rump, 4 September 1650.

Relieve the oppressed, hear the groans of poor prisoners in England. Be pleased to reform the abuses of all professions... These are our desires.

Questions

1. (i) Read Source D. Explain the reference to 'a single person and Parliament'. [2]
    (ii) Read Sources F and G. What were 'tithes'? [2]
2. Identify and account for the apparent differences between Sources B and C, or Sources D and E, or Sources F and G. [4]

*3. With reference to tone and content, what can the historian learn of Cromwell's aims and methods from Sources A, B and D? [5]

4. How reliable is Source F? [4]

5. Use these sources and your own knowledge to assess whether Cromwell's aims were incompatible. [8]

Worked answer

*3. The content of these sources suggests that Cromwell was politically and socially conservative – at least at the time of these speeches – and/or that he wanted his listeners to believe that this was the case. He desires 'government by a single person and Parliament' (Source D), thus eschewing the type of system established by the Commonwealth. He is also concerned that the powers of the 'single person and Parliament' be checked by ensuring that control of the militia be 'well and equally placed' (Source D). In Source B Cromwell bolsters the impression that he was conservative by nature by stating that the hierarchical structure of society as it 'had been known for hundreds of years . . . is a good interest of the nation'. It is clear from Source A that he stresses his conservatism because he wants to advance a 'healing and settling' of the nation. Yet, Source D also provides evidence of Cromwell's radical religious intent since on this occasion he calls for religious toleration, 'liberty of conscience'.

The tone of these extracts – which is generally emotive and rather inflated – suggests that Cromwell's method on these occasions was to win support by persuasion. He makes ready use of the rhetorical question and, in Source B, employs a historical reference. On the other hand, Source D has an aggressive undercurrent, the Lord Protector simply telling his audience that liberty of conscience 'ought to be' a fundamental. This is echoed by the phrase 'I judge' in Source A. Finally, despite the importance of the speech of 12 September 1654, there is evidence that Cromwell was poorly prepared since he admits that he had 'forgotten' the militia.

SOURCES

2. IMAGES OF THE LORD PROTECTOR, OLIVER CROMWELL

Source J: Figure 2: gold crown coin minted during the reign of Charles I, 1631–1632.

a   b

The inscriptions read:

(A) CAROLVS D.G. MAG. BRIT. FR. ET HIB. REX [Charles, by the grace of God, King of Great Britain, France and Ireland]

(B) CVLTORES SVI DEVS PROTEGIT [God protects his worshippers]

(Charles I gold crown, viewed on both sides, 1631–2, the Tower Mint, London; in the Ashmolean Museum, Oxford)

Source K: Figure 3: half-crown minted from the period of Oliver Cromwell's Protectorate, 1656.

a   b

The inscriptions read:

(A) OLIVAR D.G. RP. ANG. SCO. ET HIB. &c. PRO. [Oliver, by the grace of God, Protector of the Republic of England, Scotland and Ireland etc.]

(B) PAX QVAERITVR BELLO [Peace is sought by War]

(Oliver Cromwell half-crown, viewed on both sides, 1656, the Tower Mint, London; in the British Museum)

Source L: Figure 4: the royal arms of Stuart.

Source M: Figure 5: the arms of the Protectorate.

Source N: Figure 6: a contemporary Dutch caricature of Oliver Cromwell with a crown and sceptre.

WITHAL

Courtesy: Mansell/Time Inc.

Source O: Figure 7: a royalist view of Cromwell, from the frontispiece of Perninchief's *Syracusan Tyrant*, 1661.

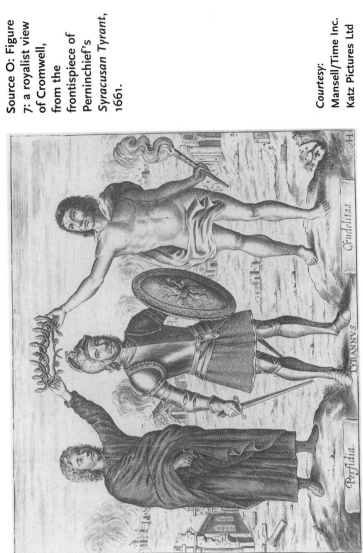

Perfidia.   TYRANNVS.   Crudelitas

Source P: Figure 8: Oliver Cromwell, an engraving by William
Faithorne the Elder (1616–1691).

Source Q: Figure 9: Oliver Cromwell standing in state, Somerset House, 1658.

Questions

1. Identify and account for the similarities and differences between either Sources J and K or Sources L and M. [4]
*2. Look at Source P. In what ways would a critic of the Lord Protector resent this portrayal of Oliver Cromwell? [7]
3. Look at Sources N and O. Which is the more effective in its appeal? [4]
4. Look at Source Q. How useful is this source for the historian? [4]
5. Use these sources and your own knowledge to assess whether Cromwell was indeed 'a King in all but name'. [6]

Worked answer

*2. A critic would regard Cromwell as the bringer of political division and unquiet. He would also hold him responsible for all the social and economic difficulties that afflicted England and the rest of Britain in the 1650s. Clearly, then, he would resent the way that the artist has portrayed Cromwell as the victor over error, faction and immorality (represented by the dying snake and female corpse) and the bringer of peace and tranquillity, represented by the dove carrying an olive branch and the full sun that has driven away the rains leaving the Ark safe and sound. Moreover, he would baulk at the suggestion – as represented by the scene of a rural idyll and bountiful harvest – that the rule of Cromwell had brought fullness and plenty. Also, the notion that Cromwell's Protectorate had ushered in a period of unity and optimism, illustrated by the crowns of the three kingdoms athwart the Lord Protector's sword would have created resentment.

On the other hand, a critic would welcome the artist's portrayal of Cromwell as essentially a military man (he is heavily clad in armour) and the suggestion that his power is dependent upon the support of the army (as shown by the depiction of musketeers and pikemen). However, nowhere is there any sign of a breakdown of religious order or evidence of the effects of groups such as the Ranters. This is something that the critic would probably wish to add.

7

FOREIGN POLICY DURING THE PROTECTORATE OF OLIVER CROMWELL, 1653–1658

BACKGROUND NARRATIVE

By the time that Oliver Cromwell was installed as Lord Protector on 16 December 1653 the Anglo-Dutch War had been raging for eighteen months. For two main reasons it is not surprising that these two republican regimes engaged in hostilities. First, there existed in England a concern that the House of Orange harboured pro-Stuart sympathies. Second, economic rivalry between the two countries was great and growing. When the Dutch failed to abide by the terms of the Navigation Act of 1651 – stipulating that goods imported into England should henceforth be carried either in English ships or in ships belonging to the country of origin – there began a war that was to last until the Dutch were defeated and forced to agree terms for peace according to the terms of the Treaty of Westminster in April 1654. At the same time, Cromwell formed a treaty with Sweden providing for peace and commerce. To this was added an agreement with Denmark in September instituting a political alliance.

Bolstered by both the outbreak of peace and a commercial agreement formed in July 1654 with Portugal – an enemy of Spain

– Cromwell now took offensive action against the traditional English foe, Catholic Spain. In December of 1654 a total of thirty-eight ships and 6,000 men set sail for the West Indies in order to attack Spain in her colonies, particularly San Domingo in Hispaniola. However, the 'Western Design' met with disaster, capturing only Jamaica (later useful for sugar and slaves) and prompting Philip IV of Spain to declare war on the Protectorate. Now engaged in war with Spain, it was all the more important that the Protectorate encouraged the continuation of hostilities between that country and France. To this end, recognising that France was a greater threat than Spain, and with his prejudices appeased by the fact that this Catholic country provided toleration to its Protestant inhabitants (the Huguenots), Cromwell formed a defensive agreement with France in November 1655. In March of 1657 this was turned into an offensive alliance against Spain, the Lord Protector agreeing to provide 6,000 men and a fleet to join 20,000 French troops for a campaign in Flanders.

The decision to ally with France had two effects in particular. First, it forced Charles II to ally with Spain (2 April 1656). However, not only was Spain increasingly weak but Charles II's association with England's traditional enemy did little to enhance the popularity of his cause. Second, following the success of an Anglo-French force on 14 June 1658 at the Battle of the Dunes, the Protectorate obtained possession of Dunkirk – an important Channel port that was retained until 27 October 1662 when it was purchased by France for £300,000.

ANALYSIS: WHAT CONSIDERATIONS DETERMINED THE FOREIGN POLICY OF OLIVER CROMWELL'S PROTECTORATE? WAS HIS FOREIGN POLICY AN ANACHRONISM?

Historical opinion has divided not only over the domestic achievements and methods of Oliver Cromwell but also in respect of the foreign policy of the Lord Protector. The older historiography of this topic, presenting a largely damning picture of events, has been criticised by such historians as Timothy Venning and Michael Roberts.[1] They argue that instead of pursuing religious interests at the cost of national and commercial concerns, Cromwell's actions were essentially pragmatic.

In a speech delivered to Parliament in January 1658 Cromwell asserted that England had undertaken a great design to stem the tide of Catholicism. He told his audience that the Catholic Habsburgs were set upon destroying the Protestant interest, that the King of Sweden, who had 'ventured all for Protestantism', was now in mortal danger and that the Jesuits were currently a greater threat than they had been in the reign of Elizabeth.[2] Such pronouncements have led historians to accuse Cromwell of having shaped his foreign policy according to criteria that were increasingly irrelevant to the circumstances of the 1650s. Seemingly obsessed with the 'Black Legend' of Spain, Cromwell appears to have been possessed of an attitude more suited to the Elizabethan age than his own. As a result, it has been alleged that economic and even security considerations were sacrificed on the altar of ideology. Yet, while Cromwell was preoccupied with outworn prejudices, the leaders of other countries – notably the Protestant Scandinavia – were coming to recognise that their interests might best be served even if it meant attacking a nation that professed the same religion. Others, such as Protestant Sweden and Catholic France, furthered their respective interests by forming alliances that were non-confessional in nature. In such circumstances Cromwell's foreign policy does indeed appear anachronistic and, according to Slingsby Bethel, 'carried him on to all his mistakes and absurdities, to the irreparable loss and damage of the famous kingdom'.[3]

Nor does the evidence appear to be slight in support of such a view. For instance, according to the terms of the Treaty of Westminster of April 1654 Cromwell brought to a conclusion the war that had been raging with the Protestant Dutch since 1652. Even though England had enjoyed the upper hand against the enemy, routing the enemy's fleet in the battle of Texel on 31 July 1653, in which the Dutch Admiral Tromp was killed, and capturing over 1,400 sail, including 120 men-of-war throughout the whole course of the war, at least one historian considers that the terms of peace were 'extraordinarily mild'.[4] Indeed, the peace treaty did not impose any meaningful restrictions upon Dutch trade and freedom of navigation and thus prompted bitter attacks from the mercantile community. 'Make wars with Dutchmen,' exclaimed a popular jingle, 'Peace with Spain / Then we shall have Money and Trade again.'[5] Cromwell's leniency appears to be explained by the fact that he sought to induce the Dutch to form an alliance with Britain in order that the two nations might simultaneously renew the war against Spain. Yet it was hardly likely that the Dutch would show any eagerness to renew a war from which they had escaped only five years previously (the Treaty of Westphalia, 1648). This, along with the continuing and deepening trade rivalry between the two nations, ensured that a meaningful Anglo-Dutch union would be almost impossible to achieve.

It seemed that Cromwell was 'not guilty of too much knowledge' in foreign affairs.[6]

It is also alleged that the Lord Protector's determination to erect a Protestant confederation against the Habsburgs further distorted and obscured his vision of events. In particular, he appears to have regarded Charles X of Sweden as a great Protestant champion in the mould of Gustavus Adolphus. On one occasion Cromwell informed his listeners that he considered Charles X 'as good as any these last ages hath brought forth [and] that hath adventured his all against the Popish interest'.[7] In reality the King of Sweden was driven by a joint desire to emerge victorious from a deeply rooted dynastic conflict and to further the national interest of his country by any means available. In the circumstances that prevailed in the Baltic this meant that Charles X desired Britain's help, not only to defeat the Catholic Habsburgs, but also to advance his struggle with the Protestant Danes and the Dutch for hegemony in Scandinavia.

Yet the most frequent criticism of Cromwell's foreign policy is that he was guilty of continuing to regard Catholic Spain as Britain's greatest enemy. 'Why, truly, your great enemy is the Spaniard,' Cromwell told his listeners in the Second Protectorate Parliament.[8] As a result, so it is argued, Cromwell perpetrated two grave errors. First, in the Western Design of 1655 he aimed to seize the Spanish islands of Hispaniola and Cuba in the Caribbean and thereafter embark on the conquest of mainland Spanish America itself. However, not only was the Western Design an utter failure – only Jamaica being captured – but the war spread to Europe and the plan to conquer Spanish America was thus abandoned. This in turn damaged English mercantile interests since they were henceforth prevented from being able to continue their trade with Spain and, moreover, were forced to yield that trade to the neutral Dutch. Moreover, the defeat of the hitherto invincible forces of the New Model Army was probably instrumental in encouraging Spain to declare war on Britain in February 1656. All in all, in the words of Bethel, the whole episode was 'contrary to our interests'.[9] Second, Cromwell's designs against Spain led him to form an alliance in November 1655 – consolidated in March 1657 – with that country's greatest enemy, France. This decision to ally with France prompted some later commentators to criticise Cromwell for having destroyed the balance of power between Spain and France and laying the foundations for the future greatness of France 'to the unspeakable prejudice of all Europe in general and of this nation in particular'.[10] 'J. R. Jones writes that Cromwell's policies 'were [therefore] misdirected, unrealistic and unsuccessful'.[11]

Yet this damning interpretation of Cromwellian foreign policy is the inevitable consequence of a general acceptance of the Protector's public pronouncements and owes a good deal to the advantages of hindsight. After all, in the 1650s it was not yet apparent that France, preoccupied with the Frondes and their effects – a domestic crisis that incapacitated Mazarin's government for four years, 1648–1652 – was to emerge as a greater threat than Spain to Britain's interests. This development occurred later in the century and was encouraged as much by the machinations of the restored monarchy as by any action taken by Cromwell. Moreover, it is certainly not the case that trade was consistently sacrificed in order to advance the Protestant cause. For instance, in contrast to the interpretation offered above, it has been argued recently that the peace with the Dutch in 1654 was, at least on paper, 'a remarkable triumph for the English'.[12] Amongst other things, it provided for British ownership of the island of Pula Run in the East Indies – part of the Dutch empire and a source of valuable spices – and compensation to be paid to English merchants whose trade had been damaged in the war. Nor did Cromwell fail to recognise that the Dutch continued to threaten English access to trade in the Baltic, vital as a source of timber, hemp and tar. He thus ensured that the Navigation Act – initially enacted by the Rump Parliament on 9 October 1651, stipulating that all goods brought into Britain should be carried either in English ships or in ships from their country of origin – continued to be implemented with great rigour. In 1655 a total of sixty Dutch ships were seized for contravening its terms. Cromwell also signed a commercial treaty with Sweden in 1654 in order to balance the effects of the Dutch alliance with Denmark.

Recent research, making use of Secretary of State John Thurloe's detailed memorandum of foreign policy, has also served to provide a new assessment of Cromwell's policies towards the Protectorate's most threatening neighbours, France and Spain. Far from being determined to enter hostilities with the latter, it is now clear that Cromwell aimed to maintain friendly relations with both powers for as long as possible in the hope of perpetuating the Franco-Spanish conflict. Since the Protectorate possessed an armed force of about 40,000 and the largest navy in Europe, Cromwell, by resisting pressure to form an alliance with either France or Spain, could reasonably expect each of those countries to outbid the other in the quest to win the allegiance of the Protectorate. At least partly to encourage this process, Cromwell signed a treaty with Spain's enemy, Portugal, on 10 July 1654. Even though the terms of this agreement were commercial in nature, it nevertheless encouraged Spain to offer the return of Calais if Cromwell would assist a Spanish offensive in Flanders. France, meanwhile, offered Dunkirk – eventually captured from the Spanish in the Anglo-French offensive of 1657 and gifted to the Protectorate in 1658. Possession of this valuable port denied an invasion base to Charles II. According to Thurloe, its acquisition meant that Cromwell 'carried the Keys of the Continent at his Girdle'.[13]

Although Cromwell acted in a way that suggested he would ally only with the highest bidder, he was keenly aware that France was the more dangerous threat to the Protectorate. Not only was it stronger than Spain but it had close family links with the Stuarts. However, moves towards the formation of an alliance with France ran into difficulty when, in May 1655, Duke Charles Emmanuel of Savoy – a puppet of France – suppressed a campaign by the Protestants of Piedmont to secure their religious freedom. Only after King Louis XIV had interceded with the Duke of Savoy and ensured that the rights of the Protestants in Piedmont were restored – thus preventing Cromwell from having to make a decision between political gain and religious conviction – did Britain and France sign a defensive treaty on 24 October 1655. The most significant effect of this alliance, consolidated in 1657, was that it forced Charles II to ally with the weaker of the two warring nations, Spain. The treaty that Charles II signed with Philip IV provided for the latter to supply 4,000 infantry and 200 cavalry if the Royalists seized a port for them to use, an unlikely event considering the efficiency of Thurloe's spy network. Moreover, since the agreement also provided for Charles II to assist Spain to reconquer Portugal and for the return of all English gains in the West Indies since 1630, what little popular demand there existed for a restoration of the Stuarts was likely to be further diminished. Above all, Spain proved singularly incapable of financing and equipping an invasion of England on Charles's behalf.

Even before the formation of an alliance with France, Cromwell had taken steps to enhance the security of the Protectorate. Thus, as a result of the treaty of 1654, the Dutch were obliged to refuse any help to Charles II and exclude from power the Dutch House of Orange, which had formerly provided assistance to the royal refugee. Moreover, in contrast to the older interpretation of events, Cromwell has been praised for his relations with Sweden. Michael Roberts has also pointed out that Cromwell's declarations of support for Charles X had excellent strategic motives.[14] Not only did Charles X's enemy, Jan Casimir of Poland, possess a sympathy for Charles II, but also any Swedish descent upon the Holy Roman Empire worked to Cromwell's advantage since it meant that the Emperor would be unable to provide aid to his Habsburg cousin, the King of Spain. Moreover, Roberts points out that in real terms Charles X received little support beyond volunteer soldiers and money. Indeed, even in 1655 – before Cromwell had engaged in war with Spain – the Protector ignored an appeal to send 6,000–8,000 troops to Sweden.

Considerations other than those relating to issues of religion, trade or security also helped to fashion Cromwell's foreign policy. According to the terms of the Instrument of Government, Cromwell was obliged to seek the 'advice and consent' of the Council of State. However, in 1654 this was divided into three factions, one led by John Lambert, who sought an alliance with Spain against Charles II's French allies, one led by Sir Gilbert Pickering, who urged the reverse, and the last led by Secretary Thurloe, who sought the preservation of peace with all potential enemies and the continuation of the Franco-Spanish conflict. Domestic circumstances therefore encouraged Cromwell in his policy of holding off from forming an alliance with either France or Spain in the hope that each would outbid the other in order to obtain the support of the Protectorate. Another determinant of foreign policy stemmed from the military nature of the Protectorate. Since Cromwell could not disband his armed forces because the country remained unsettled, and since the main reason for that disquiet was the high level of taxation required to pay a standing army and a navy, the only option seemed to be to press the military into active service. Not only would this keep them occupied, but it would provide a justification for asking the nation to pay for their upkeep. Furthermore, it could be hoped that a campaign like the Western Design would pay for itself from the plunder and territory it would acquire. 'It was told us', said Cromwell, that the [Western] Design would cost little more than laying by the ships, and that with great profit.'[15]

Cromwell's foreign policy was therefore determined by a mixture of considerations concerning issues of practicality, security, trade and religion. Of these, it was probably the last that was of greatest importance to Cromwell himself, though Michael Roberts believes that the key determining factor 'was not fanaticism, but fear'.[16] What is difficult to dispute is that Oliver Cromwell obtained for Britain a significance in Europe hitherto not enjoyed. As the initial international response to the new republican regime in England in 1649 had been horror combined with bewilderment, this was an achievement that was all the more impressive. Even Clarendon admitted that ultimately 'Cromwell's greatness at home was a mere shadow of his greatness abroad.'[17]

Questions

1. 'What brave things he did, and made all the neighbour princes fear him' (Pepys). To what extent do you agree with this assessment of Oliver Cromwell's foreign policy?
2. How successful was Cromwellian foreign policy?

SOURCES

1. CROMWELL'S FOREIGN POLICY

Source A: an extract from a memorandum composed during the 1660s by Cromwell's Secretary of State, John Thurloe.

I find the alliances of those times were contracted and conserved upon these interests: . . . To deprive his Majesty of foreign assistance in his restitution [restoration]. Hence it was that the alliance with France was preferred to that of Spain . . . The Protector also endeavoured a peace between the Dane and the Swede . . . [Yet] there were no greater considerations in England, in reference to foreign interests, than how to obviate the growing greatness of the Dutch.

Source B: an extract from the Swedish ambassador's account, sent to Charles X, of a conversation with Cromwell in 1655.

[Cromwell] protested his affection to Your Majesty and his earnest desire for his friendship. He then laid bare, in the greatest confidence, the fundamenta [fundamentals] of all his policies; which were directed to no other ends than *libertatem religionis* [freedom of religion] and freedom of trade.

Source C: a report by the French ambassador in England to the Comte de Brienne, 24 May 1655.

I have pressed them [the English] . . . to sign the treaty . . . But the Secretary of State . . . sent me word . . . that his Highness [Cromwell], being moved at the cries and lamentations of the poor Protestants of Savoy . . . , [and aware of] the great authority which the King hath upon the Duke of Savoy . . . , could not sign a treaty in such a rencounter [situation] as this. I confess I was surprised at this . . . I know not to what I shall attribute this proceeding, so contrary to expectation. The zeal of religion is certainly not able to shake the design of the Lord Protector.

Source D: Cromwell's responses to Lambert after the latter – during a meeting of the Council of State on 20 July 1654 – had requested that the Lord Protector justify undertaking the Western Design.

(1) Now providence seemed to lead us hither, having 160 ships swimming, most of Europe our enemies except Holland, and that would be well considered also. (2) The probability of the good of the design, both for the Protestants' cause and utility to the undertakers [entrepreneurs], and the cost no more for one twelve month than would disband the ships.

Source E: Cromwell to the Second Protectorate Parliament, 17 September 1656.

[The Spaniard] is naturally throughout an enemy; an enmity is put into him by God . . . And the Spaniard is not only our enemy accidentally, but he is providentially so . . . And truly [Spain] hath an interest in your bowels . . . The papists in England . . . have been accounted, ever since I was born, Spaniolised.

Source F: a despatch by the Venetian secretary recording the reaction of the Spanish ambassador in London to news of the attack on the island of San Domingo in April 1655.

He said no more except that he had the same experience as all the other foreign ministers here, namely, that self-interest is the sole guide to the actions of this government.

Source G: Slingsby Bethel, *The World's Mistake in Oliver Cromwell* (published 1668).

But as if the Lord had infatuated, and deprived him of common sense and reason, [Cromwell] neglected all our golden opportunities . . . Instead of advancing the reformed [Protestant] interest, [he] hath by an error in his politics been the author of destroying it.

Questions

1. (i) Read Source C. Account for the 'cries and lamentations' of the Protestants in Savoy. [2]
    (ii) Read Source D. 'Now providence seemed to lead us hither.' What was the Western Design? [2]
*2. (i) Read Sources A and B. What were the 'interests' and 'fundamenta' of Cromwell's foreign policy? [4]
    (ii) To what extent are the 'interests' and 'fundamenta' referred

to in Sources A and B confirmed by the other sources in this collection? [6]
3. Which is the more reliable for the historian researching Cromwellian foreign policy, Source A or G? [5]
4. Use these sources and your own knowledge to assess whether Cromwell's attitude towards foreign policy meant that he 'neglected all our golden opportunities'. [6]

Worked answer

*2. (i) The author of Source A mentions several 'interests'. First, he alleges that Cromwell sought to prevent the restoration of Charles II. Second, he states that Cromwell desired to effect peace between the states of Denmark and Sweden. Third, Thurloe states that Cromwell also sought to thwart the 'growing greatness' of the Dutch. Source B alleges that Cromwell aimed at achieving freedom of both religion and trade. This source also suggests that the Lord Protector hoped to achieve an alliance of some kind with Sweden. We are informed that Cromwell had an 'earnest desire' for the friendship of Charles X.

(ii) If *libertatem religionis* is taken to mean freedom for all Protestants, then it is a notion that receives support in some of the sources presented here. In Source D, for example, Cromwell remarks that he expects the Western Design to further the 'Protestants' cause'. Source G implies that Cromwell intended to advance 'the reformed interest'. Source C, in that it relates how Cromwell 'could not sign a treaty' with France while that country permitted the Duke of Savoy to repress Protestants in Piedmont, further supports the notion that Cromwell was concerned to attain religious freedom. On the other hand, the author of Source C also expresses surprise at Cromwell's attitude, asserting that 'the zeal of religion' was not the main motivating force behind the actions of the Lord Protector. Indeed, Source D, in its remark that the Western Design would be of 'utility to the undertakers', supports Source B's belief that Cromwell aimed at achieving 'freedom of trade'. It can also be inferred that the 'treaty' mentioned in Source C was designed to thwart the restoration of the Stuarts, a Cromwellian aim remarked upon in Source A. However, none of the Sources confirm Source A's assertion that Cromwell was seeking to erect some sort of Protestant confederation in the Baltic. Moreover, Source D suggests that foreign policy was in part determined as a means of avoiding the cost of disbanding the ships and Source F states that the determining factor was 'self-interest' – neither of which is mentioned in Sources A and B.

8

THE COLLAPSE OF THE REPUBLICAN EXPERIMENT, 1658–1660

BACKGROUND NARRATIVE

At some point before his death on 3 September 1658, albeit in rather mysterious circumstances, Oliver Cromwell – in accordance with the terms of the Humble Petition and Advice – nominated as his successor his eldest son, Richard. The lack of protest in England upon his accession, combined with a ready acceptance in Ireland and Scotland of the transfer of power, seemed to suggest that the protectoral regime was now firmly established. However, on 22 April 1659 the army, suspicious that it was about to suffer attacks upon its strength and independence, forced Richard to dissolve the Parliament he had first met on 27 January. By this action it effectively killed the Protectorate just as it had killed the Rump in April 1653. Yet, seemingly forgetful of how bitter relations between soldiers and MPs had become during the Commonwealth (1649–1653), the army now reinstituted the Rump. On 7 May 1659 42 of the 78 persons who were eligible to do so trudged back into the Commons. The restored Rump proved just as antagonistic to the army as it had been during its first incarnation and was therefore once again prevented from meeting by the soldiers on 13 October. Indeed, its termination would probably have come sooner if the Rump and the army had not faced a common enemy in the summer – a Royalist rising in Cheshire led by Sir George Booth. The army now instituted a Committee of

Safety composed of twenty-three civilian and military republicans and headed by General Fleetwood. Crucially, it failed to maintain the loyalty of all the armed forces. In particular, General Monck, the commander of the army in Scotland, declared for the expelled Rump – a declaration that prompted ineffective resistance from Lambert, who had marched north to confront Monck. When the fleet followed Monck's example, Fleetwood was compelled to recall the Rump on 26 December. Such was the chaos now prevailing that Monck crossed into England on 1 January 1660, seemingly to protect the Rump from acts of lawlessness. And this he did for several weeks after arriving in London on 3 February. Then, perhaps because the breakdown in law and order was greater than he had imagined, he changed his mind. Instead of continuing to support the Rump he readmitted those MPs secluded from Parliament by Pride's Purge on 6 December 1648, the effect of which was to overwhelm those inclined to a republic. The restored Long Parliament dissolved itself on 16 March, having first arranged elections for its successor. This latter – called the Convention Parliament since it convened itself – opened on 25 April 1660. On 1 May it received the Declaration of Breda from Charles II, a document in which Charles offered a general pardon, liberty to tender consciences, the provision of military arrears and stipulated that Parliament should have the right to resolve any disputes over land ownership. (Indeed, throughout the Declaration Charles is careful to anticipate a role for, and intimate his respect of, Parliament. There was also a significant omission: no space was given to the monarchical prerogative.)

Thus, pushed by the anarchy at their backs and pulled by the irresistible appeal of Charles, on 5 May 1660 Parliament resolved 'that the government was and ought to be by Kings, Lords and Commons'. The Interregnum was at an end.

ANALYSIS: IDENTIFY AND EXPLAIN THOSE FACTORS THAT ACCOUNT FOR THE RESTORATION OF THE STUART MONARCHY IN 1660.

Historians have been unable to agree upon the moment from which a restoration of the Stuarts became a likely event.[1] On the one hand, it has been argued that the origins of the Restoration were deep-rooted, that the execution of Charles I was no more than a spasm of revolutionary fervour. Thereafter, according to this view, the conservative forces inherent in seventeenth-century society compromised and ultimately overwhelmed any radical momentum. Certainly the 1650s witnessed a reactionary process: rule by a single-chamber Parliament from 1649 to 1653 (the Commonwealth) was supplanted by government by a single person and Parliament from 1653 to 1658 under two successive written constitutions of different origins. From this perspective, what is perhaps surprising is not that the Interregnum eventually failed but that it lasted so long. Alternatively, Austin Woolrych has cautioned against accepting the view 'that conservative reaction went so far under the Protectorate that the transition from Oliver Protector to Charles Rex did not make so very much difference'.[2] Indeed, until the early months of 1660 there was little enthusiasm for a restoration of the Stuarts. Significantly, a Royalist rebellion that was planned on a nationwide basis for the summer of 1659 managed to raise only a small force in Cheshire under Sir George Booth.

Nor did the death of Oliver Cromwell on 3 September 1658 result in the onset of disorder and disquiet, circumstances that may in turn have produced demands for the return of Charles II. 'All things are quiet in the City,' noted a newsletter writer.[3] The army appeared cowed and quiescent and Thurloe's spy network effectively hobbled the underground Royalist organisation, the Sealed Knot. Meanwhile, addresses of congratulation flooded in to Richard so that by the end of the year the new Lord Protector had received at least twenty-eight from the counties and twenty-four from towns. Moreover, the peaceful succession of Oliver's eldest son to the title of Lord Protector seemed to suggest that the new written constitution, the Humble Petition and Advice, was working. Nor was Richard either the 'Queen Dick' or the 'Tumble-down Dick' as depicted in the various tracts put about by his enemies after his fall but instead exhibited real political ability, demonstrated by the way in which he handled demands from the army that he relinquish his position as commander-in-chief: he made Fleetwood Lieutenant-General with immediate control of the army while himself retaining the supreme power, the granting of commissions. Clarendon, commenting on events in 1658, remarked that 'the King's condition never appeared so hopeless [or] so desperate'.[4]

Nevertheless, there were certainly serious unresolved problems inherent in the regime bequeathed by Oliver, not least continuing constitutional divisions and an increasingly weak financial position. Yet they alone are insufficient to explain the speed of the collapse of the Protectorate and the subsequent Restoration. Within eight months of his accession, Richard had been toppled, a victim not of the reactionary processes of the 1650s, but of the radical forces that had been kept in check only by the person of Oliver Cromwell.

Richard had inherited a regime that rested on an increasingly narrow base of support. On the one extreme were the Royalists who could, of course, never reconcile themselves to a republican regime. On the other extreme were the civilian republicans, men such as Sir Arthur Haselrig, Sir Henry Vane the younger, Thomas Scot and Edmund Ludlow. These so-called Commonwealthsmen believed that government should be by a single-chamber Parliament and therefore resented what they perceived to be Oliver's betrayal of what they called the Good Old Cause – a reference to the period of government without a single person having ultimate control, 1649–1653. Ominously, in the final few days of January 1658 a petition inspired by the Commonwealthsmen had circulated in the City, demanding the abolition of the Protectorate and the Other House and the restoration of a single-chamber Parliament. It was killed only by Oliver's dissolution of Parliament on 4 February 1658. Alongside the Commonwealthsmen were military republicans, soldiers who were increasingly reluctant to accept the recent direction of events. John Lambert, the author of the Instrument of Government, was forced to resign his commission as major-general in the summer of 1658 after refusing to swear an oath of allegiance to Oliver as required by the Humble Petition and Advice. As recently as 11 February 1658 Oliver had cashiered six officers – including William Packer, the commander of his own regiment of horse – because they refused to withdraw their view that the Cromwellian Protectorate had departed from the Good Old Cause. Thus, after the spring of 1657 the only positive support for the Protectorate came from the group responsible for sponsoring the Humble Petition, 'civilian Cromwellians' like Edward Montagu, Charles Howard, Sir Charles Wolseley, Viscount Fauconberg, Nathaniel Fiennes, Bulstrode Whitelocke, Sir Thomas Widdrington and Lord Broghill. Yet, when Oliver turned down the offer of the Crown even these men retracted their support, albeit temporarily. Nor had the radical sects any reason to be enamoured with the regimes of the 1650s for they had retained tithes and failed to provide religious freedom to all Protestants.

The regime that Richard inherited was therefore based on little more than passive acquiescence, a situation that could alter fatally if the Lord Protector was obliged to make unpopular demands of his subjects. Any such regime could be held in place by the support of the army, but a large standing army necessitated substantial tax demands which in turn further alienated support from the regime. Nor could this situation be avoided by borrowing for there was no Bank of England in the 1650s and other creditors were losing confidence in the ability of the republic to repay its debts. Thus, by the end of 1658 England's annual deficit was more than £500,000, while army arrears stood at £890,000. In total, the Protectorate was in debt to the tune of nearly £2.5 million, whereas its annual income was only £1.4 million. These were circumstances that were set to destabilise, with devastating effect, all the republican regimes 1658–1660.

In order to secure more revenue Richard was obliged to call the Third Protectorate Parliament which met on 27 January 1659. Inevitably, this provided a platform to the Commonwealthsmen, who refused to recognise Richard as Lord Protector and called for the repeal of the Humble Petition and Advice. An attack from any single element opposed to the Protectorate might have been overcome for its effect would probably have driven the other factions into support of the Protector. However, when MPs voted to restrict the army's involvement in politics, to limit toleration and then began to debate settling the army as a militia the effect was to force an alliance between the Commonwealthsmen on the one hand and the sects and the soldiers on the other. When Richard sought to fragment their unity by attempting to disband the Council of Officers, the army Grandees, Fleetwood and Desborough, mobilised the soldiers and forced Richard to dissolve Parliament on 22 April. Shortly afterwards, the Lord Protector resigned and retired into private life. Richard has been blamed for this outcome, accused of having relied too heavily upon the civilian Cromwellians and failing to realise that his power in fact depended upon the soldiers. While this may be true, the real blame for Richard's failure must be directed at his father. Too late in the day had Oliver introduced his eldest son to politics and hardly at all to the army.

The fall of the Protectorate marked the beginning of the end of the Interregnum, though it must have seemed otherwise to contemporaries. Indeed, with the army now in sole command the most likely scenario was that a republican form of government would be assured and lasting. However, the soldiers found it impossible to fashion a stable government. Over the course of the next eight months they recalled the Rump in May 1659, replaced it with a Committee of Safety in October and then recalled the Rump once again in December. Clearly, the civilian and military republicans found it impossible to work together. Extraordinarily, the restored Rumpers picked up where they had left off in 1653 and began a series of actions that indicated to their creators, the army, that they saw the Protectorate – which, in its form according to the Instrument of Government, was an army-devised constitution –

as a meaningless interval that had been forced upon them. Nor were matters helped by the animosity that existed between Haselrig and Lambert, now back at the centre of events. Yet, not only were there divisions between the army and the Rump but within each of these elements. Haselrig and Vane, for instance, were increasingly at odds. Meanwhile, the army was riven by various factions. For instance, after the dissolution of Richard's Parliament, Fleetwood supported the continuation of the Protectorate but was eventually obliged to appease the demands of the rank and file and restore the Rump. Above all, the commander of the forces in Scotland, General Monck, could not bring himself to agree with the Council of Officers' decision to dismiss the Rump in October 1659. Against this background, as G. E. Aylmer has observed, 'no one defeated the English republicans; they destroyed themselves'.[5]

Nevertheless, the internecine quarrelling of the republicans does not, of itself, explain the restoration of the Stuarts. After all, the civilian Cromwellians may have yet hoped to command sufficient support to re-found a Protectoral-type regime, with perhaps Monck at its head. However, so intense was the quarrelling of the republicans that it precipitated a fundamental breakdown in law and order. In the autumn of 1659 London witnessed serious anti-army riots and a refusal by merchants to pay taxes until a 'free' Parliament was summoned. Events deteriorated yet further when the law courts ceased to function. Ominously, Lambert's rank and file let it be known that they would not join a fight themselves but would be 'happy to make a ring' in which their officers could set upon each other. The City goldsmiths began moving out of the capital and news sheets spoke of 'shops shut, trade gone, fears and jealousies multiply'.[6] These circumstances, exacerbated by a series of poor harvests after 1657, encouraged a growth in the number of religious radicals, especially the Quakers who numbered perhaps as many as 60,000 in 1659. Their propensity to preach naked, combined with their refusal to pay tithes, take oaths, use titles or doff their hats to a superior, meant that the Quakers were particularly alarming to the propertied members of society. All these developments induced an intensely conservative reaction among the latter and fomented a popular demand for the restoration of the monarchy.

Nevertheless, the nature of *the* Restoration of 1660 can only be fully understood by examining the actions of Charles II and George Monck, the commander-in-chief of Scotland who enjoyed the support of an apolitical army numbering 10,000.

Monck – of whom 'never was more said, and less known' – reacted to the appeal for help from Haselrig by declaring for the Rump in late

October 1659 and thereafter moving his forces to the English border.[7] His action had a number of effects. In the first instance it made worse the breakdown in law and order because the Council of Officers responded to Monck's declaration by sending Lambert to Newcastle, thus bringing events to the brink of another civil war. Second, it encouraged the navy to declare for the Rump and soldiers garrisoned at Portsmouth to mutiny in its favour. These were pressures that Fleetwood could not withstand and he therefore restored the Rump for a second time on 26 December. However, by far the greatest significance of Monck in terms of explaining why there was a restoration is his conclusion that the Rump was not up to the job: it was not providing stable government. Thus, on 21 February 1660 Monck effected a reversal of Pride's Purge, readmitting those MPs secluded on 6 December 1648 on condition that they voted to dissolve the Long Parliament and organise fresh elections. Thereafter, it was inevitable that Charles II would be invited to return, a prospect made yet more palatable because – acting in accordance with Monck's advice – Charles had relocated his court from the hated Spanish Netherlands to the Protestant port of Breda.

However, it was by no means inevitable that Charles would be restored without first being obliged to agree to certain conditions, perhaps like those that his father had been offered at Newport in 1648. There were two main reasons why this did not occur. First, there was a palpable concern among some MPs that if Charles's restoration was made conditional then he might be frightened off, thus jeopardising the prospects for settlement. Second, other MPs who were demanding the imposition of conditions were persuaded that such action was unnecessary by the Declaration of Breda. In this Declaration, the timing and terms of which are accounted for by the influence of Monck and Edward Hyde, Charles eased the consciences of the as-yet hesitant MPs by offering an irresistible package designed to bind up 'those wounds which have so many years together been kept bleeding'.[8] Its four main clauses promised: to grant a general pardon to all except those specifically excepted by Parliament; to declare a liberty to tender consciences; to leave the resolution of disputes over land ownership to Parliament; and to provide the soldiers with payment of their arrears. The Convention Parliament therefore resolved on 5 May 1660 'that the government was and ought to be by Kings, Lords and Commons'.[9] The Cavalier spirit had indeed broken out 'very high'.

The collapse of the Interregnum was therefore induced by a number of factors: the nature of Oliver's financial and political legacy, the mistakes of Richard, the actions of Monck, the political bankruptcy of both the Rump and the army and the detrimental effects of a string of poor harvests. Yet the mere collapse of the republic did not make a restoration of the Stuarts inevitable. After all, there were alternatives, such as the creation of a new Protectoral regime or the installation of King Monck. However, the factors listed above conditioned the *nature* of the collapse of the republic and ensured that it would be an anarchic affair. To those possessed of property it was therefore a matter of some urgency that a stable form of government be devised, and the example suggested from history was that it should be a monarchy. That it should be the Stuart monarchy was because it had only recently been deposed and there was an adult king available in the person of Charles II; that it should be the monarchy as it stood in 1641 was because of the way that Charles and his advisers fashioned his appeal in relation to the circumstances of 1660.

Questions

1. At what point did the Restoration become inevitable?
2. To what extent did Charles II owe his restoration to events that were outside his control?

SOURCES

1. THE BREAKDOWN IN LAW AND ORDER, 1658–1660

Source A: from Thomas Rugg's diurnal (the seventeenth century equivalent of a collection of newspaper cuttings), 1659–1661.

In the morning [of 5 December 1659] the apprentices began to appear in a disorderly manner ... [and so] the Committee of Safety ... ordered that some regiments of horse and foot should forthwith march into the City ... In their march ... there was many affronts offered and a great many of uncivil actions ..., especially to Colonel Hewson['s] regiment of foot ... [Hewson] had but one eye, but [the apprentices] called him blind cobbler, blind Hewson, and did throw old shoes and old slippers and turnips tops, brickbats and stones and tiles at him and his soldiers ... Among the rude multitude there were some [that] did fire a pistol at the soldiers and some that threw great stones at the soldiers, that did very much kindle wrath [so] that at last they fired in earnest, and four or five of the apprentices and others ... were killed and others wounded, and likewise of the army very dangerously wounded. But this action was done contrary to the orders of the Lord Mayor and Court of Aldermen.

Source B: from a pamphlet written by the Quaker Dorothy White in 1659.

Upon the 25th day of the second month 1659 as I was passing along the street, I heard a cry in me . . . The word of the Lord came unto me, saying *write, and again I say write* . . . O you bloodthirsty rulers of England, you rule by the powers of darkness . . . The power of God . . . is come to turn the world upside down. That which hath rule over may be brought down and that which hath been of low degree may be raised by the power of God to rule and have dominion.

Source C: from the autobiography of the wife of a Yorkshire gentleman, written in 1707 recalling the events of 1659–1660.

About this time we were all in great confusion in this kingdom . . . In this distraction each man looked upon [each] other strangely, none knowing whom to trust, or how to be secured from the rage, rapine and destruction of the soldiery . . . And we had all suffered so deeply under those oppressions . . . that most sober, wise people of this nation began to have a good opinion of the ancient government of this realm.

Source D: from *History of My Own Time* (1723) by Bishop Gilbert Burnet.

Upon Richard's leaving the stage, the Commonwealth was again set up: and the Parliament which Cromwell had broke was brought together: but the army and they fell into new disputes, so they were again broke by the army: and upon that the nation was like to fall into great convulsions . . . and it made many conclude it was necessary to call home the King, so that matters might again fall into their old channel.

Source E: from the Declaration of Breda, 4 April 1660.

If the general distraction and confusion which is spread over the whole kingdom doth not awaken all men to a desire and longing that those wounds which have so many years been kept bleeding may be bound up, all we can say will be to no purpose.

Questions

1. Read Source D. (i) When was the Commonwealth period and what were its defining features? [2]
   (ii) Explain the reference to 'the Parliament which Cromwell had broke'. [2]
2. Of what value are Sources A and D to the historian studying

the collapse of the Interregnum? Is one more reliable than the other? [5]

3. How effectively does the author of Source B make use of language in order to emphasise her message? [4]

4. In the context of Sources A to D, what can a historian learn about the style and aptitude of Charles II from Source E? [4]

*5. Use these sources and your own knowledge to assess whether the 'distraction and confusion' (Source E) of this period is sufficient a factor to explain the Restoration of 1660. [8]

Worked answer

*5. Each of the Sources A to D describes aspects of the 'distraction and confusion' that is referred to in Source E, though only two of them assert directly that 'the rage, rapine and destruction' (Source C) created circumstances that facilitated the Restoration. Source C insists that the 'great confusion in this kingdom' encouraged people to seek the restoration of the Stuarts, 'to have a good opinion of the ancient government of this realm'. This is supported by Source D's depiction of a fear of 'great convulsions' creating a demand 'that matters might again fall into their old channel'. Sources A and B do not remark upon any such direct connection between the breakdown of law and order and a conservative reaction, but it can be inferred that the factors to which they relate – 'uncivil actions' of the 'rude multitude' and the fact that 'God . . . is come to turn the world upside down' – are fundamental in any explanation of the reactions described in Sources C and D.

These sources are therefore important in helping to explain why Charles II was invited back to Britain. Yet it would be unwise to accept them at face value. Source C, for example, is clearly biased in its description of those who supported a restoration as 'sober, wise people'. In addition, both Sources C and D were written (or at least published, in the case of D) a considerable time after the events they describe, thus raising concerns as to the accuracy of their accounts.

Moreover, these sources are helpful only in explaining why a restoration occurred. They are insufficient in terms of explaining the nature of the Restoration of 1660. It is therefore necessary to be aware of other factors not mentioned in the sources. In particular, the way in which Charles II cleverly enhanced his appeal meant that the majority of MPs in the Convention Parliament were persuaded to restore him without conditions. Their consciences were eased by the royal

Declaration of Breda which offered a general pardon, liberty to tender consciences, the provision of arrears to the soldiers and the leaving of the resolution of disputes over land ownership to Parliament.

SOURCES

2. GENERAL GEORGE MONCK

Source F: an extract from Monck's speech, Edinburgh, 15 November 1659.

Having a call from God and his people to march into England . . . I do here authorise you [members of the political nation] to suppress all tumults, stirrings and unlawful assemblies, and that you hold no correspondency with any of Charles Stuart's party or adherents, but apprehend any such as shall make any disturbance, and send them into the next garrison.

Source G: extract from a letter from the King to Monck, 10 May 1660.

You cannot but expect that there are many persons still contriving the same mischiefs against me and you, and who must be rather suppressed by your authority and power than won and reconciled by your indulgences. And it may be a little severity towards some would sooner reduce the rest than anything you can else do.

You may be most confident, and I do again renew my promise to you, for the performance of which you may engage your life, that I will make good whatever you have found necessary to promise to those of your Army who have and shall adhere to you to make your business the more easy.

Source H: from Clarendon's *History*.

The general, upon the perusal of the copies of the several despatches [from the King], liked all very well. And it ought be remembered for his honour, that from this time [21 February 1660, the day that the secluded members were readmitted to Parliament] he behaved himself with great affection towards the King; and though he was offered all the authority that Cromwell had enjoyed, and the title of King, he used all his endeavours to promote and advance the interest of his majesty.

Source I: an extract from Thomas Skinner's *Life of General Monk* (published 1723).

By his prudence he baffled all his enemies, and unravelled all the labyrinths of their crooked subtlety. By the same virtue he preserved to himself the continued affection and kindness of his Majesty, which shone upon him to the evening of his life without the interruption of the least cloud.

Source J: Robert Wild, *Iter Boreale*, 1660.

> George was wary; his cause did require
> A pillar of cloud as well as fire.

Questions

1. Read Source F. Explain the reference to 'any of Charles Stuart's party of adherents'. [2]
2. Suggest other types of evidence not present in this collection of sources that may help the historian provide a fuller assessment of Monck. [3]
*3. Is it likely that Monck will have 'liked all very well' the contents of the King's letter, Source G? [4]
4. Which of the sources, H, I or J, is likely to be the most reliable for the historian researching the methods of Monck? [6]
5. (i) In what main way do Sources G and H contradict the content of Source F? [2]
   (ii) Use Sources I and J and your own knowledge to explain this contradiction. [8]

Worked answer

*3. (This question does not demand a particularly long answer but it is essential that the response has a firm sense of balance supported with precise detail.)

On the one hand it appears that Clarendon's assertion is likely to have been correct. Certainly Monck will have been pleased by the King's assurance that he will 'make good' whatever Monck had felt it 'necessary' to do/give in order to maintain the allegiance of the soldiers. However, on the other hand, the General may have baulked at the King's criticism of his methods. In the first part of Source G the King tells Monck that 'mischiefs' will continue unless he uses his 'authority and power' rather than 'indulgences'. It is a theme that Charles reiterates by informing Monck that 'a little severity towards some' – therefore suggesting that he has not used any such hitherto – would provide a good example to all.

NOTES AND SOURCES

1. THE BACKGROUND TO THE CRISIS OF 1637–1640

1. Quoted in C. Russell: *The Crisis of Parliaments, English History 1509–1660* (Oxford University Press, 1981), p. 310.
2. See J. P. Kenyon (ed.): *The Stuart Constitution, Documents and Commentary* (Cambridge University Press, 1980), pp. 85–86.
3. K. Sharpe: *The Personal Rule of Charles I* (Yale, 1992), p. 585.
4. Edward Hyde, Earl of Clarendon: *History of the Rebellion and Civil Wars in England*, W. Dunn Macray (ed.), 6 vols (Oxford University Press, 1888), vol. I, p. 190 (Book II, § 89). (Hereafter, Clarendon, *History*.)
5. Printed in J. P. Kenyon (ed.): op. cit., p. 482.
6. Quoted in C. Carlton: *Going to the Wars: The Experience of the British Civil Wars, 1638–1651* (Routledge, 1992), pp. 28–29.
7. M. C. Fissel: *The Bishops' Wars: Charles I's Campaigns against Scotland 1638–1640* (Cambridge University Press, 1994), p. 225.
8. Quoted in C. Carlton: op. cit., p. 29.
9. Quoted in M. C. Fissel: op. cit., p. 206.
10. Quoted in K. Sharpe: op. cit., p. 800.
11. C. Russell: *The Causes of the English Civil War* (Oxford University Press, 1990), p. 163. (Hereafter, *Causes*.)
12. Quoted in M. C. Fissel: op. cit., p. 84.
13. Quoted in ibid., p. 117.
14. Quoted in ibid., p. 115.
15. J. S. Adamson: 'England without Cromwell,' in N. Ferguson (ed.), *Virtual History: Alternatives and Counterfactuals* (Papermac, 1997), p. 99.
16. C. Russell: *Causes*, p. 155.
17. Quoted in J. P. Kenyon (ed.): op. cit., p. 201.
18. Quoted in C. Russell: *The Fall of the British Monarchies 1637–1642* (Oxford University Press, 1991), p. 131. (Hereafter, *Fall*.)

19. Quoted in C. Carlton: op. cit., p. 28.
20. Quoted in C. Russell: *Causes*, p. 120.
21. Quoted in K. Sharpe: op. cit., p. 821.
22. The Petition is printed in S. R. Gardiner (ed.): *The Constitutional Documents of the Puritan Revolution* (Oxford University Press, 1906), pp. 134–136. (Hereafter, *Constitutional Documents*.)

Source A: Quoted in K. Sharpe: op. cit., p. 888.
Source B: Quoted in C. Carlton: op. cit., p. 28.
Source C: Quoted in K. Sharpe: op. cit., p. 892.
Source D: Quoted in ibid., p. 889.
Source E: Quoted in ibid., p. 891.
Source F: Quoted in ibid., p. 893.
Source G: Quoted in ibid., p. 893.
Source H: E. S. Cope and W. H. Coates (eds): *Proceedings of the Short Parliament of 1640*, Camden Society, 4th series, vol. XIX, RHS, 1977, p. 139.
Source I: Ibid., p. 141.
Source J: Ibid., pp. 242–244.
Source K: Printed in J. P. Kenyon (ed.): op. cit., p. 210.
Source L: E. S. Cope and W. H. Coates (eds): op. cit., p. 114.

2. THE EMERGENCE OF ROYALISTS AND ROUNDHEADS, 1640–1642

1. See C. Russell: 'Parliamentary History in Perspective, 1604–1629,' *History*, 61, 1976, pp. 1–27 and Richard Cust and Anne Hughes: 'Introduction, After Revisionism,' in R. Cust and A. Hughes (eds): *Conflict in Early Stuart England: Studies in Religion and Politics 1603–1642* (Longman, 1989).
2. C. Russell: 'The British Problem and the English Civil War,' reprinted in C. Russell: *Unrevolutionary England* (Hambledon Press, 1990), p. 244.
3. See J. Morrill: 'The Causes of Britain's Civil Wars,' reprinted in J. Morrill: *The Nature of the English Revolution* (Longman, 1993), pp. 252–272.
4. Quoted in A. Fletcher: *The Outbreak of the English Civil War* (Arnold, 1981), p. 12.
5. S. R. Gardiner (ed.): *Constitutional Documents*, pp. 163–166.
6. Both of these documents are printed in J. P. Kenyon (ed.): op. cit., pp. 226–240.
7. Quoted in A. Fletcher: op. cit., p. 150.
8. D. L. Smith: *Constitutional Royalism and the Search for a Settlement, c. 1640–1649* (Cambridge University Press, 1994), p. 7.

9. The speech is reprinted in J. P. Kenyon (ed.): op. cit., pp. 19–20.
10. Quoted in M. C. Fissel: op. cit., p. 56.
11. A remark made by James I at a meeting with the Puritans at Hampton Court in 1604.
12. Quoted in C. Russell: *Fall*, p. 247.
13. G. E. Aylmer: *Rebellion or Revolution? England from Civil War to Restoration* (Oxford University Press, 1986), p. 20. (Hereafter, *Rebellion or Revolution?*)
14. A. Fletcher: op. cit., p. 14.
15. C. Russell: *Causes*, p. 15.
16. See C. Russell: *Fall, passim.*
17. J. S. A. Adamson: 'Parliamentary Management, Men of Business and the House of Lords, 1640–1649,' in C. Jones (ed.): *A Pillar of the Constitution* (Hambledon, 1989), p. 31.
18. S. Lambert: 'The Opening of the Long Parliament,' *Historical Journal*, 27 (2), 1984, p. 285.
19. See J. Morrill: 'The Unweariableness of Mr Pym: Influence and Eloquence in the Long Parliament,' in S. Amussen and M. Kishlansky (eds): *Political Culture and Cultural Politics in Early Modern England* (Manchester University Press, 1995), pp. 19–54.
20. J. H. Hexter: *The Reign of King Pym* (Harvard, 1941), p. 200.
21. For the speeches of April and November 1640 see J. P Kenyon (ed.): op. cit., pp. 197–205.
22. Quoted in C. Russell: *Causes*, p. 15.
23. C. Russell: *Fall* p. 333.
24. V. Pearl: *London and the Outbreak of the Puritan Revolution: City Government and National Politics, 1625–1643* (Oxford University Press, 1964), p. 230.
25. Quoted in C. Russell: *Fall*, p. 294.
Source A: R. Ellis: *People, Power and Politics: Was There a Mid-seventeenth Century English Revolution?* (Stanley Thornes, 1992), p. 103.
Source B: Ibid., p. 104.
Source C: C. Daniels and J. Morrill (eds): *Charles I* (Cambridge University Press, 1988), p. 95.
Source D: J. P. Kenyon (ed.): op. cit., pp. 228–229.
Source E: Clarendon, *History*, vol. I, p. 222 (Book III, § 3).
Source F: J. P. Kenyon (ed.): op. cit., p. 207.
Source G: R. Ellis: op. cit., p. 101.
Source H: J. P. Kenyon (ed.): op. cit., p. 241.

3. THE WAR MACHINES, 1642–1646

1. I. Roy: 'The Royalist Council of War: 1642–1646,' *Bulletin of the Institute of Historical Research*, 35, 1962, pp. 150–168.
2. Quoted in C. Holmes: *The Eastern Association in the English Civil War* (Cambridge University Press, 1974), p. 85.
3. S. R. Gardiner (ed.): *Constitutional Documents*, pp. 249–254.
4. Printed in H. Tomlinson and D. Gregg (eds): *Politics, Religion and Society in Revolutionary England, 1640–1660* (Macmillan, 1989), p. 67.
5. Quoted in V. Snow: *Essex the Rebel* (Nebraska Press, 1970), p. 357.
6. Clarendon, *History* vol. II, pp. 106–111 (Book V, § 202–205).
7. J. Morrill: *Revolt of the Provinces* (Longman, 1980), p. 40. (Hereafter, *Revolt.*)
8. R. Hutton: *The Royalist War Effort* (Longman, 1982), p. 83. (Hereafter, *War Effort.*)
9. J. Morrill: *Revolt*, p. 114.
10. R. Hutton: *War Effort*, p. 52.
11. Quoted in J. Morrill: *Revolt*, p. 52.
12. The Petition was drawn up by the Commons in 1628. According to its terms, MPs sought the King's agreement not to raise taxation without Parliament's consent, imprison any of his subjects without showing cause, billet troops on civilians without their consent, or impose martial law on civilians.
13. Quoted in I. Gentles: *The New Model Army in England, Ireland and Scotland, 1645–1653* (Blackwell, 1992), p. 93. (Hereafter, *New Model.*)
14. C. Hill: *The World Turned Upside Down* (Temple Smith, 1972), p. 46.
15. Printed in D. L. Smith (ed.): *Oliver Cromwell, Politics and Religion in the English Revolution 1640–1658* (Cambridge University Press, 1991), pp. 72–73. (Hereafter, *Oliver Cromwell.*)
16. M. Kishlansky: *The Rise of the New Model Army* (Cambridge University Press, 1979), p. 27. (Hereafter, *Rise.*)
17. See A. Woolrych: 'Cromwell as a Soldier,' in J. Morrill (ed.): *Oliver Cromwell and the English Revolution* (Longman, 1990) p. 102.
18. See J. S. A. Adamson: 'Oliver Cromwell and the Long Parliament,' in ibid., p. 65.
19. M. Kishlansky: 'The Case of the Army Truly Stated: The Creation of the New Model Army,' *Past and Present*, 81, 1978, p. 58.
20. For details of the balance between Presbyterians and Independents see ibid., pp. 66–68.
21. These figures are in I. Gentles: *New Model*, p. 32.
22. Quoted in Kishlansky: *Rise*, p. 50.

23. C. H. Firth: *Cromwell's Army* (Methuen, 1902), p. 48.
24. Quoted in ibid., p. 46.
25. Figures in ibid., p. 46.
26. See I. Gentles: *New Model*, p. 48.
27. Quoted in ibid., p. 107.
28. Ibid., p. 115.
29. Ibid., p. 119.
30. Quoted in ibid., p. 87.
Source A: B. Coward and C. Durston (eds): *The English Revolution* (John Murray, 1997), p. 73.
Source B: Ibid., p. 69.
Source C: Ibid., p. 71.
Source D: Ibid., p. 72.
Source E: Ibid., pp. 74–75.
Source F: L. Hutchinson: *Memoirs of the Life of Colonel Hutchinson* (Everyman, 1995), p. 162.
Source G: D. L. Smith (ed.): *Oliver Cromwell*, p. 17.
Source H: Ibid., p. 16.
Source I: S. R. Gardiner (ed.): *Constitutional Documents*, pp. 287–288.

4. THE VICTORS FALL OUT AND THE EMERGENCE OF RADICALISM, 1646–1649

1. The declaration of 14 June 1647 is reprinted in J. P. Kenyon (ed.): op. cit., pp. 295–301.
2. The Propositions are reprinted in S. R. Gardiner (ed.): *Constitutional Documents*, pp. 290–306.
3. For the Heads see ibid., pp. 316–326.
4. See J. Bruce (ed.): *Charles I in 1646: Letters of King Charles I to Queen Henrietta Maria*, Camden Society, old series, vol. LXIII, 1856.
5. D. E. Underdown: *Pride's Purge: Politics in the Puritan Revolution* (Oxford University Press, 1971), p. 98.
6. Reprinted in D. L. Smith (ed.): *Oliver Cromwell*, pp. 17–18.
7. Quoted in R. Ashton: *Counter Revolution: The Second Civil War and its Origins, 1646–8* (Yale University Press, 1994), p. 25.
8. The Four Bills and Engagement are reprinted in S. R Gardiner (ed.): *Constitutional Documents*, pp. 335–352.
9. Quotes are from the Leveller Large Petition in G. E. Aylmer (ed.): *The Levellers in the English Revolution* (Thames and Hudson, 1975), p. 79.
10. H. Shaw: *The Levellers* (Longman, 1973), p. 12.
11. See note 1 of this chapter.
12. See note 3 of this chapter.

13. Quoted in P. Gregg: *Free-born John: A Biography of John Lilburn* (Dent, 1986), p. 193.
14. In C. Hill and E. Dell (eds): *The Good Old Cause: The English Revolution of 1640–1660. Its Causes, Course and Consequences* (Cass, 1969), p. 339.
15. J. S. Morrill: 'The Army Revolt of 1647,' in J. S. Morrill: *The Nature of the English Revolution* (Longman, 1993), p. 329.
16. H. Shaw: op. cit., p. 97.
17. A. Woolrych: 'Looking back on the Levellers,' *The Historian*, 34, 1992, p. 8.
18. H. Shaw: op. cit., p. 96.
19. F. D. Dow: *Radicalism in the English Revolution 1640–1660* (Blackwell, 1985), p. 51.
Source A: B. Coward and C. Durston (eds): op. cit., p. 102.
Source B: S. R. Gardiner (ed.): *Constitutional Documents*, pp. 306–307.
Source C: C. Petrie (ed.): *The Letters of King Charles I* (Cassell, 1968), pp. 205–206.
Source D: S. R. Gardiner (ed.): *Constitutional Documents*, p. 313.
Source E: A. Sharp (ed.): *The English Levellers* (Cambridge University Press, 1998), pp. 36–38.
Source F: C. Hill and E. Dell (eds): op. cit., p. 331.
Source G: L Hutchinson: op. cit., p. 222.
Source H: A. Sharp (ed.): op. cit., p. 137.
Source I: Clarendon, *History*, vol. IV, p. 261 (Book X, § 126).
Source J: A. Sharp (ed.): op. cit., pp. 103–104.
Source K: M. Slater (ed.): *Englishmen with Swords* (Merlin, 1991), p. 128.
Source L: K. Lindley (ed.): *The English Civil War and Revolution: A Sourcebook* (Routledge, 1998), p. 172.
Source M: C. Hill and E. Dell (eds): op. cit., p. 403.
Source N: A. Sharp (ed.): op. cit., p. 198.

5. THE TRIAL AND EXECUTION OF KING CHARLES I AND THE CONSTITUTIONAL CONSEQUENCES, 1649–1653

1. See J. P. Kenyon (ed.): op. cit., pp. 318–319.
2. Quoted in D. L. Smith: *A History of the Modern British Isles 1603–1707: The Double Crown* (Blackwell, 1998), p.183.
3. For a summary of these positions and their limitations see B. Coward: *Stuart England 1603–1714* (Longman, 1997), pp. 103–108.
4. Quoted in C. V. Wedgewood: *The Trial of Charles I* (Penguin, 1983), p. 193.

5. For the text of the Engagement see S. R. Gardiner (ed.): *Constitutional Documents*, pp. 347–353.

6. Cromwell to Robert Jenner and John Ashe, 20 November 1648, in *The Letters and Speeches of Oliver Cromwell, with Elucidations by Thomas Carlyle*, S. C. Lomas (ed.), 3 vols, I (London, 1904), p. 387.

7. In J. P. Kenyon (ed.): op. cit., pp. 318–319.

8. Quoted in D. Smith (ed.): *Oliver Cromwell*, p. 26.

9. For the text of the Four Bills see S. R. Gardiner (ed.): *Constitutional Documents*, p. 335–347.

10. S. R. Gardiner: *History of the Great Civil War*, IV, pp. 327–328. (Hereafter, *History*.)

11. For the text of the Vote of No Addresses see S. R. Gardiner (ed.): *Constitutional Documents*, p. 356.

12. B. Worden: *The Rump Parliament 1648–1653* (Cambridge University Press, 1974), p. 76.

13. Quoted in S. R. Gardiner: *History*, IV, p. 235.

14. For the text of the Humble Petition see J. P. Kenyon (ed.): op. cit., pp. 319–324.

15. H. N. Brailsford: *The Levellers and the English Revolution* (Spokesman, 1983), p. 350.

16. Quoted in P. Gaunt: *Oliver Cromwell* (Blackwell, 1996), p. 103.

17. Quoted in C. Hill: *God's Englishman: Oliver Cromwell and the English Revolution* (Pelican, 1970), p. 98. (Hereafter, *God's Englishman*.) Some historians, including recently John Morrill, have argued that Cromwell was convinced of the need to remove the King from much earlier in 1648 and question this traditional view that he remained reluctant and uncertain until very late in that year.

18. Quoted in S. R. Gardiner: *History*, IV, p. 288.

19. Quoted in S. R. Gardiner: *History of England from the Accession of James I to the Outbreak of the English Civil War, 1603–1642*, 10 vols, IX (London, 1883–1884), p. 341. (Hereafter, *England*.)

20. Quoted in S. R. Gardiner: *History*, IV, p. 290.

21. Quoted in D. Lagomarsino and C. J. Wood (eds): *The Trial of Charles I: A Documentary History* (University Press of New England, 1989), p. 6.

22. Quoted in ibid., p. 6.

23. Quoted in B. Manning: *1649: The Crisis of the English Revolution* (Bookmarks, 1992), p. 32.

24. The text is in J. P. Kenyon (ed.): op. cit., p. 324.

25. Quoted in S. R. Gardiner: *History*, IV, p. 300.

26. Quoted in ibid., p. 289.

27. Quoted in D. Lagomarsino and C. J. Wood (eds): op. cit., p. 80.

28. See D. E. Underdown: op. cit., chapter 8.

29. S. R. Gardiner (ed.): *Constitutional Documents*, p. 391.

30. D. Hirst: *Authority and Conflict: England 1603–1658* (Arnold, 1986), p. 297.
31. B. Worden: *The Rump Parliament* (Cambridge University Press, 1974), p. 52.
32. See A. Woolrych: *Commonwealth to Protectorate* (Oxford University Press, 1982), especially chapter 9.
33. Quoted in D. L. Smith: *A History of the Modern British Isles*, p. 183.
34. G. E. Aylmer: *Rebellion or Revolution?*, p. 158.
35. For the debate about the existence of the Ranters see J. C. Davis: *Fear, Myth and History: The Ranters and the Historians* (Cambridge University Press, 1986). Quote in D. L. Smith: *A History of the Modern British Isles*, p. 173.
36. C. Hill: *God's Englishman*, p. 148.
37. B. Worden: *Rump Parliament*, p. 69.
38. Printed in D. L. Smith (ed.): *Oliver Cromwell*, p. 38.
39. S. C. Lomas (ed.): *Cromwell's Speeches*, III, p. 336.
40. Quoted in C. Hill: *God's Englishman*, p. 137.
41. T. Barnard: *The English Republic* (Longman, 1982), p. 33.
Source A: D. Lagomarsino and C. J. Wood (eds): op. cit., p. 86.
Source B: C. Hill and E. Dell (eds): op. cit., pp. 372–373.
Source C: W. Lamont and S. Oldfield (eds): *Politics, Religion and Literature in the Seventeenth Century* (Dent, 1975), pp. 134–135.
Source D: D. L. Smith (ed.): *Oliver Cromwell*, p. 28.
Source E: Ibid., pp. 27–28.
Source F: Reprinted courtesy of Earl of Rosebery/National Galleries of Scotland.

6. THE PROTECTORATE OF OLIVER CROMWELL, 1653–1658

1. Quoted in P. Gaunt: '"The Single Person's Confidants and Dependants"? Oliver Cromwell and his Protectoral Councillors,' *Historical Journal*, 32 (3), 1989, p. 538. (Hereafter, 'Cromwell and his Councillors'.)
2. Quoted in ibid., p. 358.
3. W. C. Abbott: *The Writings and Speeches of Oliver Cromwell*, 4 vols, IV Cambridge University Press, Cambridge, Mass., 1937–1947), pp. 897–899.
4. Quoted in A. Woolrych: *The Cromwellian Protectorate: A Military Dictatorship?* (History, 1990), p. 207. (Hereafter, *Military Dictatorship*.)
5. H. N. Brailsford: *The Levellers and the English Revolution*, C. Hill (ed.) (Cresset Press, 1961).
6. P. Gaunt: 'Cromwell and his Councillors', p. 560.

7. Quoted in C. Hill: *God's Englishman*, pp. 258 and 257.
8. A. Woolrych: *Military Dictatorship*, p. 208.
9. For the terms of the Instrument see S. R. Gardiner (ed.): *Constitutional Documents*, pp. 405–417.
10. For the Humble and Additional Petitions, see ibid., pp. 447–464.
11. P. Gaunt: 'Cromwell and his Councillors', p. 546.
12. Quoted in D. L. Smith: *A History of the Modern British Isles*, p. 190.
13. P. Gaunt: *Oliver Cromwell* (Blackwell, 1996), p. 169.
14. I. Roots (ed.): *Speeches of Oliver Cromwell* (Everyman, 1989), p. 54.
15. Quoted in B. Coward: *Oliver Cromwell* (Longman, 1991), p. 127.
16. Quoted in P. Gaunt: 'Cromwell and his Councillors', p. 539.
17. Quoted in B. Coward: *Oliver Cromwell*, p. 127.
18. J. Buchan: *Oliver Cromwell* (Hodder and Stoughton, 1934), p. 459.
19. S. R. Gardiner: *History of the Commonwealth and Protectorate*, III (Longman, 1903), p. 323.
20. J. P. Kenyon (ed.): op. cit., pp. 348–350.
21. Quoted in B. Coward: *Oliver Cromwell*, p. 131.
22. Quoted in P. Gaunt: *Oliver Cromwell*, p. 161.
23. Quoted in ibid., p. 162.
24. Quoted in A. Woolrych: *Military Dictatorship*, p. 210.
25. Ibid., p. 211.
26. Ibid., p. 220.
27. G. E. Aylmer: *The State's Servants: The Civil Service of the English Republic 1649–1660* (London, 1973), pp. 314–317; A. Fletcher: 'Oliver Cromwell and the Localities: The Problem of Consent,' in C. Jones, M. Newitt and S. Roberts (eds): *Politics and People in Revolutionary England* (Oxford University Press, 1986), pp. 187–204.
28. A. Woolrych: *Military Dictatorship*, p. 217.
29. Quoted in I. Roots: *The Great Rebellion* (Batsford, 1966), p. 177.
30. A. Woolrych: *Military Dictatorship*, p. 214.
31. Quoted in B. Coward: *Oliver Cromwell*, p. 152.
32. P. Gaunt: *Oliver Cromwell*, p. 162.
33. Quoted in ibid., p. 196.
Source A: D. L. Smith (ed.): *Oliver Cromwell*, p. 75.
Source B: Ibid., p. 69.
Source C: Ibid., p. 73.
Source D: T. Carlyle (ed.): *Oliver Cromwell's Letters and Speeches* (London, 1846), pp. 555–556.
Source E: D. L. Smith (ed.): *Oliver Cromwell*, p. 31.
Source F: C. Hill and E. Dell (eds): op. cit., p. 455.
Source G: C. H. Firth: *Oliver Cromwell and the Rule of the Puritans in England* (Oxford University Press, 1961), p. 350.

Source H: B. Coward and C. Durston (eds): op. cit., p. 171.
Source I: T. Carlyle (ed.): *Oliver Cromwell Letters and Speeches*, p. 388.
Source J: D. L. Smith (ed.): *Oliver Cromwell*, p. 42.
Source K: Ibid., p. 43.
Source L: S. Friar and J. Ferguson: *Basic Heraldry* (Herbert Press, 1993), © A & C Black (Publishers) Ltd, p. 106.
Source M: Ibid., p. 111.
Source N: Mansell Collection.
Source O: Mansell Collection.
Source P: Trustees of the British Museum.
Source Q: D. L. Smith: *A History of the Modern British Isles*, p. 194.

7. FOREIGN POLICY DURING THE PROTECTORATE OF OLIVER CROMWELL, 1653–1658

1. See T. Venning: *Cromwellian Foreign Policy* (Macmillan, 1995); M. Roberts: *Cromwell and the Baltic in Essays in Swedish History* (London, 1967).
2. The text of this speech is reprinted in T. Carlyle: *Oliver Cromwell's Letters and Speeches*, pp. 743–756.
3. Quoted in C. P. Korr: *Cromwell and the New Model Foreign Policy* (UCP, 1975), p. 202.
4. C. H. Wilson: *Profit and Power* (Longman, 1957), p. 77.
5. Quoted in J. R. Jones: *Britain and Europe in the Seventeenth Century* (Arnold, 1966), p. 36.
6. Quoted in ibid., p. 34.
7. Cromwell to the second session of the Second Protectorate Parliament, quoted in T. Venning: op. cit., p. 190.
8. Quoted in D. L. Smith (ed.): *Oliver Cromwell*, p. 101.
9. Quoted in C. P. Korr: op. cit., p. 202.
10. Edmund Ludlow, quoted in T. Venning: op. cit., p. 67.
11. J. R. Jones: op. cit., p. 34.
12. R. Hutton: *The English Republic 1649–1660* (Macmillan, 1990), p. 108.
13. Quoted in C. P. Korr: op. cit., p. 205.
14. See M. Roberts: *Cromwell and the Baltic*.
15. Quoted in T. Venning: 'Cromwell's Foreign Policy and the Western Design,' *Cromwelliana*, 1994, p. 46.
16. M. Roberts: *Cromwell and the Baltic*, p. 174.
17. Quoted in C. H. Firth: *Oliver Cromwell*, p. 381.
Source A: D. L. Smith (ed.): *Oliver Cromwell*, p. 90.
Source B: Ibid., p. 91.
Source C: Ibid., pp. 96–97.

Source D: Ibid., p. 99.
Source E: Ibid., p. 101.
Source F: Ibid., p. 100.
Source G: Ibid., p. 103.

8. THE COLLAPSE OF THE REPUBLICAN EXPERIMENT, 1658–1660

1. For competing views see I. Roots: '1649–1660, The Inter-regnum,' *History Today*, May 1983, p. 47 and G. E. Aylmer: *Rebellion or Revolution?*, p. 190.
2. A. Woolrych: 'Last Quests for a Settlement, 1657–1660,' in G. E. Aylmer (ed.): *The Interregnum: The Quest for Settlement 1646–1660* (Macmillan, 1972), p. 183.
3. Quoted in I. Roots: *Great Rebellion*, p. 232.
4. Clarendon, *History*, vol VI, p. 98 (Book XVI, § 2).
5. G. E. Aylmer: *Rebellion or Revolution?*, p. 200.
6. Quoted in B. Williams: *Elusive Settlement* (Nelson, 1984), p. 112.
7. Quoted in I. Roots: *Great Rebellion*, p. 251.
8. For the full text of the Declaration see J. P. Kenyon (ed.): op. cit., pp. 357–358.
9. Quoted in P. Seaward: *The Restoration, 1660–1688* (Macmillan, 1991), p. 12.

Source A: B. Coward and C. Durston (eds): op. cit., p. 206.
Source B: Ibid., p. 209.
Source C: Ibid., p. 207.
Source D: R. Ellis: op. cit., p. 171.
Source E: J. P. Kenyon (ed.): op. cit., p. 357.
Source F: H. Tomlinson and D. Gregg (eds): op. cit., pp. 229–230.
Source G: A. Bryant (ed.): *The Letters of King Charles II* (Cassell, 1968), pp. 90–91.
Source H: Clarendon, *History*, vol. VI, p. 210 (Book XVI, § 204).
Source I: A. Browning (ed.): *English Historical Documents 1660–1714* (Eyre and Spottiswode, 1953), pp. 929–930.
Source J: I. Roots: *Great Rebellion*, p. 250.

SELECT BIBLIOGRAPHY

PRIMARY SOURCES

Comprehensive collections of primary material may be found in
J. P. Kenyon (ed.): *The Stuart Constitution, Documents and
Commentary* (Cambridge University Press, 1966); K. Lindley
(ed.): *The English Civil War and Revolution: A Sourcebook*
(Routledge, 1998); S. R. Gardiner (ed.): *The Constitutional
Documents of the Puritan Revolution 1625–1660* (Oxford
University Press, 1889) and S. C. Lomas (ed.): *The Letters
and Speeches of Oliver Cromwell with Elucidations by
Thomas Carlyle* (London, 1904). An excellent variety of pri-
mary sources relating to the career of Oliver Cromwell can be
found in D. L. Smith (ed.): *Oliver Cromwell, Politics and
Religion in the English Revolution, 1640–1658* (Cambridge
University Press, 1991).

SECONDARY SOURCES

Useful introductions to this period are B. Coward: *The Stuart
Age* (Longman, 1980); D. Hirst: *Authority and Conflict:
England 1603–1658* (Arnold; 1986), D. L. Smith: *A History of
the Modern British Isles 1603–1707: The Double Crown*
(Blackwell, 1998); and A. G. R. Smith: *The Emergence of a
Nation State: The Commonwealth of England, 1529–1660*
(Longman, 1984). A highly readable and concise overview of
events is provided by G. E. Aylmer: *Rebellion or Revolution?
England from Civil War to Restoration* (Oxford University
Press, 1986). An accessible introduction to Scottish affairs is

provided by M. Lynch: *Scotland: A New History* (Pimlico, 1991). Events in Ireland are covered by R. F. Foster: *Modern Ireland 1600–1972* (Penguin, 1988). A useful survey of the current scholarship on Charles I is M. B. Young: *Charles I* (Macmillan, 1997). Excellent biographies of Charles I are those by C. Carlton: *Charles I, The Personal Monarch* (Routledge, 1995); and P. Gregg, *King Charles I* (Dent, 1981).

A vast number of books has been published on the Civil War. Its origins are considered by C. Russell: *The Causes of the English Civil War* (Oxford University Press, 1990). A useful overview of the conflict is provided by M. Bennett: *The English Civil War 1640–1649* (Longman, 1995). For a more detailed approach see R. Ashton: *The English Civil War, Conservatism and Revolution 1603–1649* (Weidenfeld and Nicolson, 1978). For recent attempts to present a British perspective of events see M. Bennett: *The Civil Wars in Britain and Ireland 1638–1651* (Blackwell, 1997); J. R. Young (ed.): *Celtic Dimensions of the British Civil Wars* (John Donald, 1997); and P. Gaunt: *The British Wars 1637–1651* (Routledge, 1997). Some of the effects of the conflict are considered in J. Morrill (ed.): *Reactions to the English Civil War 1642–1649* (Macmillan, 1982). A useful consideration of the emergence of radicalism is F. D. Dow: *Radicalism in the English Revolution 1640–1660* (Blackwell, 1985).

A short introduction to the 1650s is provided by A. Woolrych: *England without a King 1649–1660* (Methuen, 1983). Excellent thematic biographies of Oliver Cromwell are B. Coward: *Oliver Cromwell* (Longman, 1991); and C. Hill: *God's Englishman: Oliver Cromwell and the English Revolution* (Pelican, 1970). See also J. Morrill (ed.): *Oliver Cromwell and the English Revolution* (Longman, 1990).

The foreign policy of this period has been very largely neglected, though a useful overview is J. R. Jones: *Britain and Europe in the Seventeenth Century* (Arnold, 1966). A detailed account of foreign policy in the 1650s is T. Venning: *Cromwellian Foreign Policy* (Macmillan, 1995).

INDEX

Note: Page numbers in **Bold** *refer to Background Narratives*

Abbott, W. C. 82
Aberdeen 3
Adamson, J. 6, 22
Additional Instruction (1641) 17
Additional Petition and Advice (1657) 83, 88
Adwalton Moor, battle of (1643) **31**, 34
Agitators **48**, 61
Agreement(s) of the People 53, 54, 68
Antrim, Randal McDonnell, Earl of 4, allegedly plotting with Charles I **15**
Argyll, Archibald Campbell, Earl of 4, **15**
Army Plots, first (1641), **14**, 24; second (1641), **14**, 24
army (*see* New Model Army) assessment 36, 40
Attainder 24
Aylmer, G. E. 87, 114

Bannockburn, battle of (1314) **3**
Banqueting Hall 71, 79
Barnard, T. 75
Bastwick, John **1**
Bedford bridging scheme 19
Benburb, battle of (1646) **48**
Berwick, Pacification of (1639) **3**
Bethel, Slingsby 101, 102, 107
Bishops' Wars **2–3**,

Black Legend 101
Booth, Sir George **109**, 111
Brailsford, H. N. 68, 82
Breda, Declaration of (1660) **110**, 115, 117, 119
Bristol **31**, 49
Broghill, Roger Boyle, Lord 112
Burford 55, 72
Burton, Henry **1**

Calais 103
Carisbrooke castle **65**
Casimir, Jan 104
Cessation (*see* Ireland)
Charles Emmanuel, Duke of Savoy 104
Charles I; as commander-in-chief 32; attitude to Parliament 6–7; attitude to religious reform 18, 19, 57; attitude to the law 6; deficiencies in leadership 35–36; divides opponents **47–48**, 56–57; duplicity 18, 51, 53, 67; leaves London **30**; misses opportunity to dissolve Long Parliament 20; policy in the Bishops' Wars 3, 6, 7; positive actions in the Long Parliament 17–18; refuses to accept advice 4; stubborn 50, 51; surrenders to the Scots **47**; trial and execution 65–79, 111; unable to afford mercenaries 5

Charles II 73, **100**, 104, 105, 108, **110**, 111, 114, 115, 116, 118, 119
Charles X 102, 104, 105, 108
Cheshire **109**, 111
Clarendon, Edward Hyde, Earl of 3, 5, 21, 27, 34, 59, 76, 105, 111, 115, 119
Clubmen 35
Commissions of Array 32, 34
Committee of Both Kingdoms 32, 33, 40
Committee of Safety 32 (1642); **109–110**, 113, 116 (1659)
Commonwealth 111
Commonwealthsmen 112, 113
Convocation 6
Cony, George 84
Corkbush Field 54
Council of War (royalist) 32, 34, 36
Covenanters 3, 4, 49 alliance with Parliament 36 (1643); their demands **2**; effect of their presence in England 18–20, 23, **48**; invasion of 1640 6; religious grievances 49; revolution in Scotland 19
Cromwell, Oliver 37, 38, 61, 62, 66, 67, 69, 76, **80**, 119 aims 89–90; as Lord Protector 82–88, 91–98; aspects of character 74, 82, 84; attack on Manchester 34, 45; attitude to the army 105; battle of Preston **64**, 66; at Burford 72; cashiering of officers 112; death of **81**, **109**, 111 expulsion of Rump **65**; failure to prepare Richard 113; forms treaties with Dutch, Sweden, Denmark, Portugal, France **99–100**, 102; impact of Self-Denying Ordinance 39; in Ireland and Scotland 73; installed as Lord Protector **99**; legacy of 112, 115; and Providence 69; regicide 79; speeches to Second Protectorate

Parliament 100–101, 102, 107
Cromwell, Richard **109**, 111, 112, 113, 115, 117
Cropredy Bridge, battle of (1644) 32
Cuba 102

debt 113
decimation tax **81**, 85
Denmark **99**, 103, 108
Desborough, John 85, 87, 113
Diggers 72
Dow, F. D. 56
Dunbar, battle of (1650) 38, 73
Dunes, battle of (1658), **100**
Dunkirk **100**, 104
Dutch, the 102, 103, 104, 108
Dutch War, the 74, **99**, 101

Eastern Association 33, 40
Edgehill, battle of (1642) **30**, 33
Edinburgh **3**
Ejectors 87
Engagement (1647) 51, **64**, 66, 67
Engagement, Act (1650) 72
Engagers 49
Englands Birth-Right Justified 52
Englands Lamentable Slaverie 52
English Devil 84
episcopacy 85
Essex, Robert Devereux, Earl of 25, **31**, 33, 34, 37, 40, 45, 69

Fairfax, Lady 70
Fairfax, Sir Thomas **31**, 34, 35, 37, 40, 54, 67, 68, 69, 72, 74
Fauconberg, Thomas Belasyse, Lord 112
Fiennes, Nathaniel 112
Fifth Monarchists 73
Fissel, M. C. 4
Five Members 21, 30
Fleetwood, Charles 87, **110**, 111, 113, 114, 115
Fletcher, A. 87
Four Bills (1647) 51, **64**, 67

France **100**, 102, 103, 104, 108
Frondes, the 103

Gangraena 55
Gardiner, S. R. 67, 85
Gaunt, P. 84, 88
Gentles, I 41
Glasgow Assembly (1638) **2**
Good Old Cause **81**, 112
Government Bill (1654–1655) **80**
Grand Remonstrance **15**, 17, 20
Grandees **48**, 49, 53, 54, 113
Gustavus Adolphus, King of
    Sweden 102

Hale, Sir Matthew 74
Hamilton, James Hamilton, Marquis
    of 3, 7, 9, 49, **64**, 67
Hampden, John **1**
Harrison, Thomas 71
Haselrig, Sir Arthur 112, 114
Heads of the Proposals (1647) **48**,
    50, 53, **65**
Henrietta Maria **30**
Hill, C. 38
Hirst, D. 72
Hispaniola **100**, 102
Hitler 82
Holdenby (Holmby) House 50
Holland **65**
Holland, Henry Rich, Earl of 3
Holles, Denzil 73
Hopton, Sir Ralph 32
Hotham, Sir John 30
Howard, Charles (later Earl of
    Carlisle) 112
Huguenots **100**
Humble Petition (1648) 68
Humble Petition and Advice
    (1657) **81**, 83, **109**, 111,
    112, 113
Hurst castle 68
Hutton, R. 34. 35

Incident, the (1641) **14–15**
Independents 33, 38, 39, **48**, 49,
    50, 51, 53, 66, 67, 68, 79
Instrument of Government (1653)
    80, 83, 84, 105, 112, 113
Ireland **65**; Cessation (1643) **31**,

35; Confederates **31**, 35;
    rising of 1641 **15**, 20
Ireton, Henry 54, 61, 62, 66, 68,
    69

Jamaica **100**, 102
Jesuits 101
Jones, J. R. 102

Kelso 3
Kishlansky, M. 39, 41

Lambert, John **80**, 83, 87, 105,
    110, 112, 114, 115
Langport, battle of (1645) 37, 38,
    49
Lansdown, battle of (1643) **31**
Laud, William, Archbishop of
    Canterbury 1, **2**, **14**, 17
Leslie, Alexander (Earl of Leven) 3,
    4
Levellers 38, **48**, 51–56, 58–63,
    64, **65**, 66, 72
Lilburn, John 52, 53, 54, 55, 62
Lockyer, Robert 52
London 32, 37, 68, **110**, 114
London, treaty of (1641) 20, 23
Lostwithiel, battle of (1644) **31**,
    32, 33, 38
Louis XIV, King of France 104
Ludlow, Edmund 112

Magna Carta 84
Major-Generals, the **81**, 85, 87
Manchester, Edward Montagu, Earl
    of 34, 37, 39, 40, 45, 50
Marston Moor, battle of (1644) **31**,
    34, 36
Marten, Henry 66
Mazarin, Cardinal 103
Merchant Adventurers 52
Mercurius Politicus 85
militia 4, 33, **48**
Moderate 52, 70
Monck, George **110**, 114, 115,
    119–121
Montagu, Edward 112
Montrose, James Graham, Marquis
    of **31**, 35–36, 37, 39
Morrill, J. 16, 22, 34, 35, 55

Muggletonians 73
Mussolini 82

Nantwich, battle of (1644) **31**, 35
Naseby, battle of (1645) **31**, 37,
    38, 49
National Covenant (1638) **2**
Navigation Act (1651) **99**, 103
Naylor, James **81**
New Model Army **31**, 35–36, 37,
    38–42, **47**, **48**, 49, 53, **64**,
    69, 102
Newark **31**, 49
Newburn, battle of (1640) 3, 4, 5
Newbury, second battle of (1644)
    31, 34
Newcastle-upon-Tyne 3, 9, 50,
    115
Newcastle Propositions (1646) **48**,
    49, 67
Newcastle, William Cavendish, Earl
    of 32, 34
Newport, treaty of **65**, 67, 115
Nineteen Propositions (1642) 33
Nominated Assembly (*see*
    Parliaments)
Nottingham **30**

O'Neill, Sir Phelim **15**
Orange **99**, 104
Ormonde, James Butler, Earl of **31**,
    35
Overton, Richard 52, 58
Overton, Robert 84

Packer, William 112
Parker, Henry 36
Parliaments: Convention (1660)
    110, 118; First Protectorate
    80; Long (1640–1648 and
    1660) **14**, 16–21, **110**, 115;
    Nominated Assembly (1653)
    65, 71, 72, 75; Parliament of
    1628–1629 **1**; Rump
    (1648–1653 and
    1659–1660) **65**, 66, 69, 103
    109, **110**, 113, 114, 115,
    116; Second Protectorate
    (1656–1658) **81**; Short
    (1640) 5, 6, 10–12; Third

Protectorate (1659)**109**, **110**,
    113, 114
Penruddock, John **80**, 86, 88
Pepys, Samuel 106
Petition of Right (1628) 36, 125
Philip IV, King of Spain **100**, 104
Philiphaugh, battle of (1645) **31**,
    36, 49
Pickering, Gilbert 105,
Piedmont 104, 108
Poland 104
Popish Plot **3**
Portsmouth 115
Portugal **99**, 103, 104
Presbyterian church settlement **47**,
    49, 50
Presbyterians, (political) 33, 39,
    48, 49, 51, 53, 67, 68, 73
Preston, battle of (1648) 38, **64**,
    66
Pride's Purge **65**, 66, 69, 75, 79,
    110, 115
Prynne, William **1**
Publick Intelligencer 85
Putney Debates 53, 54, 61
Pym, John **14**, **15**; aims 22;
    methods 23–24, 27–28; and
    Junto in Long Parliament
    16–17, 21–24; in Short
    Parliament 7; war measures
    36

Quakers 73, 114

Rainsborough, Thomas 51, 61
Ranters 73
Rathmines, battle of (1649) 73
Recognition, the (1653) **80**, 86
Remonstrance of the Army (1648)
    68, 69
Ripon, Treaty of (1640) 18, 23
Roberts, M. 100, 104, 104–105
Rolle, Henry 84
Roundway Down, battle of (1643)
    31, 38
Rupert, Prince 36
Russell, C. 5, 6, 16, 20, 21, 23

San Domingo **100**, 107
Scot, Thomas 112

Scotland **65**
Scottish Prayer Book **2**
Sealed Knot 111
Self-Denying Ordinance (1645) 37, 39, 40
Shaw, H. 56
Sidney, Algernon 69
Skippon, Philip 87
Solemn League and Covenant (1643) **31**, 36, **47**
Spain **99–100**, 101, 102, 103, 104, 105
Stalin 82
Strafford (*see* Wentworth, Sir Thomas)
Sweden **99**, 101, 103, 104, 105, 108

Ten Propositions, the (1641) 16
Texel, battle of (1653) 101
Thurloe, John 82, 103, 104, 105, 106, 108, 111
tithes 52, 54, 73, 112, 114
Toleration Act (1650) 73–74
torture 86
trained bands 37
Triers 87
Tromp, Admiral 101
Turnham Green (1642) **31**, 33, 37

Underdown, D. 50
Uxbridge Propositions (1645) 39

Vane, Sir Henry, the younger 112, 114
Venning, T. 100
Verney, Sir Edmund 4
Vote of No Addresses 51, **64**, **65**, 67

Waller, Sir William 34
Walwyn, William 52, 55
Wentworth, Peter 84
Wentworth, Sir Thomas, Earl of Strafford **2**, 5, 7, 9, **14**, 24, 69; execution 17, 20; impeachment charge 11; attainted 16; Irish army, 4
West Indies, the **100**, 104
Western Design, the **100**, 102, 105, 108
Westminster, treaty of (1654) **99**, 101
Westphalia, treaty of (1648) 101
Whigs 66
Whitelocke, Bulstrode 83–84, 112
Widdrington, Sir Thomas 84, 112
Wildman, John 52
Winstanley, Gerrard 72
Wolseley, Sir Charles 112
Woolrych, A. 55, 86, 87, 88, 111
Worcester, battle of (1651) 38, 73
Worden, B. 67, 72, 74

Britain and her Empire at War
The reasons why Abergavenny was at
the centre of invasions.